THE WARRIOR

THE WARRIOR

A DEVOTIONAL GUIDE FOR DISTINCTIVE CHRISTIAN LIVING

RICK CALLOWAY

Copyright © 2019 by Rick Calloway.

Library of Congress Control Number:		2019912175
ISBN:	Hardcover	978-1-7960-5385-2
	Softcover	978-1-7960-5384-5
	eBook	978-1-7960-5383-8

All rights reserved. No part of this book may be reproduced or transmitted in any form or by any means, electronic or mechanical, including photocopying, recording, or by any information storage and retrieval system, without permission in writing from the copyright owner.

Scripture quotations marked NLT are taken from the Holy Bible, New Living Translation, copyright © 1996, 2004, 2007. Used by permission of Tyndale House Publishers, Inc. Carol Stream, Illinois 60188. All rights reserved. Website

Any people depicted in stock imagery provided by Getty Images are models, and such images are being used for illustrative purposes only.
Certain stock imagery © Getty Images.

Print information available on the last page.

Rev. date: 08/20/2019

To order additional copies of this book, contact:
Xlibris
1-888-795-4274
www.Xlibris.com
Orders@Xlibris.com
801686

Introduction

It is with great excitement that we publish this devotional. The focus of this devotional is to proclaim that distinctive Christian living is possible in all areas of our life. The ability to live this way is found in a personal relationship with Jesus Christ and by daily trusting and following Him in all we do. It is my prayer that God will use this devotional to fan the flames of your personal commitment to God so that you might be fully surrendered to Him with your life.

Contents

Chapter 1	Raising Children	1
Chapter 2	The Blessings of God	26
Chapter 3	God's Plan	36
Chapter 4	What Matters!	50
Chapter 5	Distinctive Living	56
Chapter 6	Difficult Times	73
Chapter 7	Success	89
Chapter 8	A Passion for the Lord	93
Chapter 9	What the World Needs Now!	100
Chapter 10	Choosing Wisely	109
Chapter 11	Prayer	117
Chapter 12	The Power of the Word	126
Chapter 13	Real Commitment	130
Chapter 14	Struggles We All Face	143

Chapter 1
Raising Children

Appreciating the Gift of Children

"Children are a gift from the Lord; they are a reward from Him. Children born to a young man are like arrows in a warrior's hands. How joyful is the man whose quiver is full of them!" Psalm 127:3-4

One of the greatest gifts the Lord has ever given me was my three daughters. In the busyness of life, it is easy to forget just how precious a gift from God our children are. Now that my children are grown, I am reminded just how much I have appreciated these great gifts from God. Psalm 127:3-4 gives us some powerful reasons to appreciate the gift of children.

First, the Psalmist reminds us here that they are a reward from God. A reward is something you should enjoy. My wife and I have always tried to enjoy our children. We wanted to spend as much time with them as we could when they were growing up.

Occasionally, I love to look back at old pictures and remember the days when they were little. What fun times we had while they were growing up. My wife and I always wanted to create a home in which laughter permeated our times together. That same sense of fun is still such a big part of our lives even now that they are grown.

Next, to appreciate any gift, I believe we must use it as it was intended. God intended for us as Christian parents for us to raise **"warriors"** that will impact our culture for Christ. We as parents should desire to point our children towards a lifelong love relationship with Jesus Christ. I can think of no better way to appreciate what the Lord has done in our lives through our children than to give them back to Him to use for His glory.

C.S. Lewis once said: *"Nothing that you have not given away will ever be really yours."* I believe that this holds true of children as well.

My wife Karen and I have prayed as parents over the years that God might truly use our kids to bring glory to God. I believe that is the essence of what the Psalmist is saying about our children *"being arrows in a warrior's hands."* I am convinced that God has great plans for our children and those plans include living a life that will not only bring honor and glory to God but also living a life that will accomplish great things for Him!

Finally, the Psalmist reminds us of *"how joyful is the man whose quiver is full of them."* I am grateful that God is giving us this opportunity as parents to truly appreciate the gift of children. Personally, I have been blessed to experience the joy that the Psalmist speaks of as I have watched my girls grow in the Lord and be used by Him.

May God truly bless you as appreciate the gift of children from the Lord!

What Goal Do We Need to Have for Raising Kids?

"We will not hide these truths from our children we will tell the next generation about the glorious deeds of the L<small>ORD</small>*, about His power and His mighty wonders. For He issued His laws to Jacob; He gave His instructions to Israel. He commanded our ancestors to teach them to their children, so the next generation might know them—even the children not yet born and they in turn will teach their own children.*

> *So each generation should set its hope anew on God, not forgetting His glorious miracles and obeying His commands."*
> *Psalm 78:4-7*

As my wife and I raised our children, we regularly sought God for how to do the difficult job of a parent and more importantly determining our goals. What would really be the best things we could do for our kids as they were growing up? As a parent, we are faced with so many choices that impact the raising of our children and their future. I believe that all of us face the pressure as parents to do the right thing for our children.

Psalm 78:4-7 is a great passage for helping us to find the goals we, as followers of Christ, need to have for raising our children. This passage reminds us of the main goals that God has in mind for this process. First, God is instructing us to intentionally teach the truths of God to our children. Our goal should be to teach them of **"His power and His mighty wonders."** The goal is to teach and live out our faith in such a way that it becomes a legacy of faith that will be passed to future generations of our family.

The ultimate goal is found in the phrase: **"So each generation should set its hope anew on God, not forgetting His glorious miracles and obeying His commands."** God's goals are not the goals that this world would have for our kids to find peace, joy, and truly what is best for them in this life.

I ran across something that Dr. Glen Schultz wrote a few years back that provides a great perspective on choosing what is best for our children. His wisdom in choosing not what is good for our children but what is best goes as follows:

Seek not what is important, but what is essential.

Seek not glamour, but godliness.

Seek not a place that gives your children opportunities to socialize; seek first that which gives your children opportunities for servant hood.

Seek not to increase their fun; seek to increase their faith.

Seek not tools to make them rich: seek first to give them tools to make them righteous.

Seek not what makes your kids happy; seek first what makes your kids holy.

Seek first the Kingdom of heaven and His righteousness, and then sit back and claim God's promise that every single thing your children needs to fulfill God's perfect plan for their lives will be given unto them.

God gave my wife and I the wisdom years ago to chase His goals for our children. God has continually blessed this decision in our lives over the years and returned to us so much more in who our children are in Christ than we could have ever imagined. I pray that the wisdom from Psalm 78 and Dr. Schultz will be a blessing to you as you parent your children and make the difficult choices that you make on behalf of your children each day.

One of the Greatest Gifts We Can Give Our Children

"So again I say, each man must love his wife as he loves himself, and the wife must respect her husband."
Ephesians 5:33

We spend a lot of time and money trying to figure out what kind of gifts to give our children each year. It is natural for us as parents to want to do good things for them. However, I have learned that the best gifts we can give our kids do not cost money. One of the greatest gifts we can give our children is a loving marriage with our spouse. Unfortunately, this is one thing that does not happen like it always should.

In fact, research tells us a lot about the state of marriage in America. A recent report states that there is one divorce approximately every 36 seconds. That's nearly 2,400 divorces per day, 16,800 divorces per week and 876,000 divorces a year. The average length of a marriage that ends in divorce is eight years.

It is too bad that many marriages in America are divided and many are in daily turmoil. I have counseled with so many people over the years who have confided in me that they have **"fallen out of love"** with each other. I have never understood what that means exactly. I do know that God intended for us to love our spouse in the way He prescribes.

How are we supposed to love our spouse? For me, Ephesians 5:25-26 says it all: **"For husbands, this means love your wives, just as Christ loved the church. He gave up His life for her to make her holy and clean, washed by the cleansing of God's word."**

For husbands, we are to love our wives as Christ loved the church. How did He love the church? He gave His life for the church. He gave sacrificially to the church. We are to do the same for our spouses.

I always desired something greater out of marriage. I have been blessed to be married to the love of my life for 31 years. I echo something Andy Stanley said: **"There are men who make history, there are men who change the world, and there are men like me that simply find the right girl."**

I also know that God has commanded us as followers of Christ to approach marriage so differently than the world. In Ephesians 5:33,

Paul instructs husbands to love their wives like they do themselves and for wives to respect their husbands.

Outside of the truth of God's Word, the greatest advice I ever received on marriage came from my dad. He told me that one of the greatest gifts I could ever give my children was to love their mother.

Have we positioned our marriages to leave this kind of gift for our children? May God bless each of you as you seek to live out a Godly marriage in front of your children!

Equipping Our Kids to Face the Battles of Life

2 Corinthians 7:5: "When we arrived in Macedonia, there was no rest for us. We faced conflict from every direction, with battles on the outside and fear on the inside."

"There are really two major obstacles all parents face in teaching their children to obey: not only is the world they live in corrupt, but they themselves are sinful creatures too. They face a difficult struggle both inside and outside."
-John MacArthur

I used to love to ride my bike when I was a kid. In those days, we never wore protective gear such as helmets or knee pads. At age 12, I fell off my bike and broke my arm. Today, we equip our children with knee and elbow pads, helmets, and gloves to ride their bikes to protect them from falls. These kids look like soldiers because of all the protective gear they have on. We go to great lengths to protect children against physical injuries, but do we take any precautions in regards to their spiritual protection?

When our children are little, it is important to teach them Biblical principles such as to be kind to one another and to teach them the importance of sharing. As our kids begin to grow, we need to develop a more detailed spiritual plan that will equip them to face the battles on the outside that Paul described in 2 Corinthians 7:5. A great detailed battle plan is found in Ephesians 6:11-18.

"Put on all of God's armor so that you will be able to stand firm against all strategies of the devil. For we are not fighting against flesh-and-blood enemies, but against evil rulers and authorities of the unseen world, against mighty powers in this dark world, and against evil spirits in the heavenly places.

Putting on the armor of God is one of the most important Biblical principles we can teach our children. If they are to be victorious in their Christian life, putting on the armor of God daily will be essential. From this passage, what are we to teach our children?

- ➢ Their battle is not with people. It may seem like it at times. However, I wanted to teach my kids to love others and recognize that problems and disputes occur between people but learn not to take things out on people we are upset with. I want to teach them to be quick to forgive and ask for forgiveness. I want them as they grow up to know where the real source of our problems comes from.
- ➢ I want them prepared through a study of God's Word how to use the Bible as their sword to deal with the conflicts, disputes, and problems that come their way. Knowing God's Word and hiding it in their heart will provide them with the tools necessary for the battle.
- ➢ I want them to own their faith boldly as their helmet of protection. Knowing that they are a child of the King will provide them much needed security for the battle.

> I want to teach them to be filled with the Spirit so that they will readily share the Good News, sense the peace of God, and know the comfort of truth.

Parents, prepare your children for the battles of life with teaching them the principle of putting on the armor of God.

You Never Know Who Is Watching

"Don't worry that your children never listen to you; worry that they are always watching you."-
Robert Fulgham

Our children do spend a lot of time watching who we really are. They look intently to see what we value, what we celebrate, and what we live for. I have come to realize that the greatest calling of my life is to pass a Godly heritage of faith to my children. My wife and I have worked hard at trying to teach our kids the things of God every hour that they are awake. We have sought to model a Biblical lifestyle at home, take them to church, and then to provide them with a Christian education so that their worldview would be constantly shaped by God's truth. In essence, I wanted to so model my love and pursuit of living for Jesus so that my kids who are watching would desire the same.

Modeling and living a lifestyle is important but we must also then begin to prepare our children to live for Jesus in this difficult culture. Derek Kenan said in regard to this that we should be **"teaching our kids to swim beyond the buoys."** Isn't that what we want in the final analysis? We must plan for our children to leave the confines of our homes, churches, and schools prepared to meet the rough currents of workplaces and the open hostility found on most college campuses.

How do we do this? We do this by ensuring that our children are being influenced with a Biblical Worldview so that they will learn themselves to live with such a worldview. We must begin early to make sure that our children's underlying belief system is rooted and grounded in God's Word and not the philosophies of this world. I want to give you a few verses that illustrate the importance of ensuring our kids have the right influence.

First, Proverbs 3:5-6 tells us: **"Trust in the LORD with all your heart and lean not on your own understanding; in all your ways acknowledge him, and he will make your paths straight."** If we want our children to have the right path for life, then we must teach them that their hope is in Christ Jesus alone.

Next, Luke 2:52 tells us: **"And Jesus grew in wisdom and stature, and in favor with God and men."** The greatest model to follow in raising our children is Jesus. He was raised with the priorities of wisdom, stature, favor with God and favor with man. Achieving these four goals for our children is impossible outside of the influence of God's Word and God's people.

Also, Luke 6:40 teaches us: **"A student is not above his teacher, but everyone who is fully trained will**

be like his teacher." God's Word is clear in this passage that our children will become like those who teach them and have influence on them.

Finally, Colossians 2:8-9 declares, **"See to it that no one takes you captive through hollow and deceptive philosophy, which depends on human tradition and the basic principles of this world rather than on Christ."** We do all we can to guard against our children being taken captive as these verses declare by the philosophies and principles that do not line up with God's Word.

For these very reasons, my wife and I have always prioritized Christian education for our kids. We wanted them in an environment that would influence them to develop a Biblical Worldview. We knew that they would be watching those who have influence and we made sure that they were influenced daily with God's truth. As I look back, it has been the greatest investment of our lives!

What is the Purpose of Disciplining Your Kids?

"Now no chastening for the present time seemed to be joyous, but grievous: nevertheless afterward it yielded the peaceable fruit of righteousness unto them which are exercised thereby."
Hebrews 12:11

What a promise from God that even though disciplining is not a lot of fun, it will produce clear Biblical direction for our children that will benefit them forever. From my experience, I never have enjoyed disciplining my children as Paul describes in this verse. It was never a joyous occasion. However, if you understand what this verse says you will readily see it as not only necessary but fruitful. Paul says that it will yield the peaceable fruit of righteousness.

Wait a minute! Is that not what we as Christian parents want for our kids? Our goal should be to raise Godly, righteous children. Rick, are you saying that discipline is essential to accomplishing this goal? No, I am not saying that, God is!

God gave us the model in Luke 2:52 for how Jesus was raised. Following the model of how Jesus was raised we want our children to **"*grow in wisdom, stature, favor with man, and favor with God.*"** Hebrews 12:11 reminds us that discipline is an essential part of us achieving this model for our kids.

What should be the Biblical goals for discipline? The Biblical goals for discipline line up with helping us to instill the goals of wisdom, stature, favor with man, and favor with God.

First, discipline will enable them to gain favor with man and God by learning a proper attitude and respect for authority. Second, it should help them to grow in stature and favor with God and man by requiring them to take responsibility for what they have done. Next, it should draw them into favor with God and man by teaching them to accept the consequences of their actions. It will also seek to gain them favor with God and man through correcting a defiant heart.

Following a Biblical model for discipline will also produce wisdom, discernment, and direction in the lives of our children. Hebrews 5:14 tells us that **"those who by reason of use have their senses exercised to discern both good and evil."** In other words, one of the goals we should desire for our children is that they would be good and Godly decision makers. One cannot distinguish between right and wrong without the guidance that discipline brings. You need look no further than our world today to see a generation of people who clearly do not know the difference between right and wrong.

Deuteronomy 12:8 provides a great description of this generation when it says that **"every man was doing whatever is right in his own eyes."** Biblical discipline in the lives of our kids will help to instill that level of wisdom, discernment, and direction in their lives.

As you can see, discipline is not just something we do out of anger or frustration. Discipline has a clear purpose and that purpose is to produce righteousness in our children.

Raising Our Kids with A Goal in Mind

"Children are not a distraction from more important work. They are <u>the most Important work</u>."
C.S. Lewis

Recently, I read an interesting survey of parents on how they decide what activities and commitments their family will participate in. The survey found that 54% of all parents will decide to do activities or pursue commitments if they are good for developing their children's character. 46% of parents surveyed stated that they made the decisions based on whether it makes their kids and family happy.

It is good that most parents still believe that character development should be the top criteria for how we raise our children. But clearly, many people do not have an intentional plan for accomplishing character development in their children.

In our world, the most successful companies have a mission statement and execute their activities around that mission statement. For example, Walmart's mission statement is:

"Saving people money so they can live better."

When you observe Walmart's marketing strategy or visit their stores, you can clearly see they operate by that mission statement and have been quite successful in doing so over the years. I believe the same type of principle holds true when it comes to raising our children. God's Word has provided us with a clear mission as to how to raise our kids with a goal in mind.

Proverbs 22:6 instructs us *"to train up a child in the way he should go and when he is old he will not depart from it."* This verse has a clear goal in mind that our children would be raised to follow and love God in such a way that it provides them a faith that would sustain them and last a lifetime.

Do we have a goal in mind when it comes to raising our children? Are we too focused on making them happy? Are we too focused on sports achievements, activities, and achieving worldly success?

As Christian parents, God is wanting us to be focused on raising our children to love, pursue, and follow God the rest of their lives. Yes, I do believe that He would have us as parents develop a mission statement for our families that reflects this pursuit of God and character development so that we do not get caught up in chasing things in this world that have no significance.

God Himself had a plan on how Jesus was to be raised and it is found in Luke 2:52. That verse says: *"Jesus grew in wisdom and in stature and in favor with God and all the people."* The focus for Jesus was to grow in wisdom, stature, favor with God, and favor with man. That is a solid plan that we could use with our children to ensure that they would be trained *"in the way they should go"*. I pray that all of us as parents would begin to develop an intentional plan for raising our kids to follow God with an eternal end in mind!

Practical Advice for Disciplining Our Kids

"Discipline your children and they will give you peace of mind and will make your heart glad."
Proverbs 29:17

Discipline is not an activity that we enjoy as parents. What makes it even more difficult is knowing how to discipline. This is an area I struggled with early on as a parent. During those days, we sought the Lord for advice on how to effectively discipline our kids and making sure that the punishment fit the crime.

Through time with the Lord, God gave my wife and I the wisdom to put discipline into two categories as a tool for when and how to discipline my children. The first category is what I would call "**deliberate disobedience**." That is when our children deliberately do something they know to be wrong. This type of disobedience I believe requires a more severe approach in our disciplinary approach.

The question of what we should do with deliberate disobedience is the subject of much debate today. Many today believe that spanking is harmful and will damage a child's self-esteem.

What does the Bible say about this issue? Let me give you two verses.

> - *Proverbs 23:13:" Don't fail to discipline your children. They won't die if you spank them."*
> - *Proverbs 22:15: "A youngster's heart is filled with foolishness, but physical discipline will drive it far away."*

These verses tell us that it is necessary and helpful to discipline and at least consider spanking our children. I will say as disclaimers that spanking is a punishment designed for younger ages and that we should never spank when we are mad. Regardless, deliberate disobedience requires a more serious consequence.

The second category we have used is that of "**careless or irresponsible disobedience**". These are times when they are disobedient through careless or irresponsible acts. In these situations, I wanted to apply a punishment that fit the crime.

For instance, my wife and I will regularly assign chores for our girls to do around the house to help their mother. On one such occasion, our daughter was not really happy with the chores that her mother gave her and as a result did not perform them well. When confronted with her effort, she began to complain and make excuses. We felt that the correct punishment would not only be to correct her sloppy work but also to add additional chores to her list.

Another example would be when our children began to drive to school. We told them that a consequence of being late to school would be a loss of driving privileges. The idea here is that we want to correct and hold our children accountable for irresponsibility. This type of disobedience requires consistency in teaching them to be responsible and careful in all they do.

You might be sitting there thinking that we were too tough on our children. One of the goals we have for our children is to learn to be responsible while they are young so that one day they may not have to suffer the consequences of irresponsibility by getting fired on the job.

My prayer is that my children will be responsible and trustworthy young women who bring honor and glory to God with the way they live. These traits will not happen by osmosis. It will require much prayer, much teaching, and corrective discipline.

Nobody Enjoys This!

"No discipline is enjoyable while it is happening—it's painful! But afterward there will be a peaceful harvest of right living for those who are trained in this way."
Hebrews 12:11

There just seems to be a lot of things in life that are necessary for us but at the same time are not very enjoyable. For me, I have never liked going to the dentist. I know it is necessary for good teeth health, but I would rather do just about anything than go to the dentist.

One of those areas that most parents do not enjoy is that of discipline. Why is it necessary? Are there Biblical goals for doing this unpleasant but necessary thing? If so, what should be the Biblical goals for discipline? Let's address these issues with Scripture.

Hebrews 12:11 is a promise from God that even though disciplining is not a lot of fun, it will produce clear Biblical direction for our children that will benefit our children forever. From my experience, I never have enjoyed disciplining my children as Paul describes in this verse. It was never a joyous occasion. However, if you understand what this verse says you will readily see it as not only necessary but fruitful. Paul says that it will yield the **"peaceable fruit of righteousness."**

Wait a minute! Is that not what we as Christian parents want for our kids? Our goal should be to raise Godly, righteous children. Mr. Calloway, are you saying that discipline is essential to accomplishing this goal. No, I am not saying that God is! The purpose or the why of discipline is spelled out in Hebrews 12:11 and that is to help us raise Godly, righteous children.

Following a Biblical model for discipline will also produce wisdom, discernment and direction in the lives of our children. Hebrews 5:14 tells us that **"Solid food is for those who are mature, who through training have the skill to recognize the difference between right and wrong."**

In other words, one of the goals we should desire for our children is that they would be good and Godly decision makers. One cannot distinguish between right and wrong without the guidance that discipline brings.

You need look no further than our world today to see a generation of people who clearly do not know the difference between right and wrong. Deuteronomy 12:8 defines this generation when it says that **"every man was doing whatever is right in his own eyes."**

Biblical discipline in their lives will help to instill that level of wisdom, discernment, and direction in their lives.

As you can see, discipline is not just something we do out of anger or frustration. Discipline has a clear purpose and that purpose is to produce righteousness in our children. In coming articles, I will address the dangers of not disciplining and provide practical and Biblical guidelines for disciplining.

I pray that these truths from God's Word will help us all understand why we need to discipline our children even though it is something no one enjoys doing!

How Can We Protect Our Kids in the World of Social Media?

"Guard your heart above all else, for it determines the course of your life."
Proverbs 4:23

The words of Solomon in Proverbs 4:23 are such a powerful statement to all of us as believers. He told us to ***"guard your heart above all else."*** I believe that this advice is not only for us as individuals, but I have also always believed that as a parent it was my job to protect the hearts of my children until they were of age.

I also believe these days of the internet and social media that the job of protecting our children's hearts has never been harder. What do we need to do to protect our children's heart in this age of technology? One of the areas that our kids need help and accountability with is that of social media. Social media has created a secret world in which our children will leave a digital footprint that could follow them the rest of their life.

Social media allows our children to create connections and interactions that are not altogether healthy. One thing that is evident about social media is that people are more likely to say things online that they would never say in person. For example, one late night show host has a regular segment entitled *"Mean Tweets"* in which being mean to others in a Tweet is celebrated. Not a great model for our kids.

Also, students do not often realize the consequences of what they are posting in what they believe is their own private world. This spring, 10 students who were previously accepted to Harvard University had their acceptances rescinded because of their online social media behavior. Colleges are indeed looking at students' social media footprints and most students do not realize it.

In addition, the idea of being secret and not accountable has also exploded inside the social media app called Snapchat. This is the app where teenagers know that their content is not available for all their *"Friends"* or *"Followers"* to see. You choose who you send messages to, and once it's viewed, it's gone forever… Or at least, it's supposed to be. However, it is all able to be recovered as some teens have found out the hard way.

The Pew Research group has found Snapchat to be a primary venue for sexting and cyberbullying amongst teenagers. Parents need to understand that kids enjoy Snapchat, because *"it is one of the only apps that is relatively private."* Even parents who do have access to their children's Snapchat are unlikely to see the messages sent and received through the app.

So, how do we guard their hearts in these areas of social media? *1) Make sure that your student is old enough and mature enough to handle a social media presence. 2) Make sure as a parent that you have access to all their accounts and can see all that they post and who posts to them. 3) Finally, do not allow them to have apps such as Snapchat where they can be involved in things you cannot see.*

Josh McDowell once stated that:

> **"I would rather put a fence at the top of a hill than an ambulance at the bottom."**

I pray that we would all put some barriers up in the areas of social media to guard the hearts of our children.

Capturing Moments

"Repeat them again and again to your children. Talk about them when you are at home and when you are on the road, when you are going to bed and when you are getting up."
Deuteronomy 6:7

Since I became a parent, it has always been my prayer that my children would grow to love the Lord and learn to follow and trust Him with all that they are. That is something that I believe most Christians want for their children. The real issue comes with how to get this desired outcome. I am sure that most of us have struggled with how to develop a strategy that will help us lead our children to Christ and then teach them daily to follow Him.

The Bible provides us with such a strategy in the book of Deuteronomy. In Deuteronomy 6:7, the Word directs us to talk about the things of God with our kids almost every hour they are awake. I believe this verse is in essence teaching us to capture the moments in life where we have the opportunity to pour into our children a Biblical Worldview. The verse even gives us such moments when it talks of bed time, being on the road, and our critical times at home such as meal times. All of these are precious times where we can spend quality discipling and loving our kids.

What do these times look like? The great part is we can all be very creative and individualistic in our approach. You can use certain times to study the Bible and pray together. You can also do as my wife and I did, and we would talk about everyday life with a Biblical Worldview perspective with our kids at these times. Current events, things we see on television, and daily life events at school make for great opportunities to talk of the things of God with our kids.

One of my favorite times of the day when I was growing up was meal time. My parents would use that time to capture moments and make memories with us. They would use it to teach truth through everyday conversation and also use it as a time to laugh and enjoy each other.

Maybe it is time to start creating some family practices that will enable you to capture precious moments with your children. For example, we always tried to protect meal time so that we would have these moments to spend with each other. Research tells us that our children are much more likely to follow our spiritual beliefs when we model and teach these truths daily.

My children are now grown and it all happened in seemed in the blink of an eye. I am so grateful that my wife and I put practices in place that enabled us to raise kids have given their hearts to God and are following Him.

I would challenge you to not miss capturing the moments that God has given you to pass on your love for the Lord to your children. As Third John 4 says: *"**There is no greater joy than to know that your children walk in truth.**"* I pray that we all will experience that joy!

Our Kids Need to See a Difference

"Then we will no longer be immature like children. We won't be tossed and blown about by every wind of new teaching. We will not be influenced when people try to trick us with lies so clever they sound like the truth."
Ephesians 4:14

We live in a day when it is difficult to know what **"Christian"** really means. A Gallup poll recently said that almost half of the people in the U.S. claim to be a Christian. Yet, research tells us that less than 10% of all Americans live with a Biblical worldview. With the shape this country is in, the meaning of what a Christian really is has changed.

I believe that the meaning has changed because most folks are not anchoring their lives firmly on the foundation of God's Word. We live in a generation that does not believe in absolute truth and are being "**tossed about with every wind of doctrine**" that Paul talked about in Ephesians.

As followers and believers in Christ, we should be challenging ourselves to live Biblically. We cannot hope to raise Godly kids without being a Biblically distinctive family. We must study God's Word, commit our lives to it, and use it as the dividing line for all decisions that we make. It truly should be the foundation upon which everything in our lives rest.

Research also tells us that parents are still the most influential people in the lives of children. To raise Godly kids, our kids must see a clear difference in how we live Biblically. Pursuing Christ and leading our families as He would have us is critical for the spiritual development of our children.

In Psalm 63, David declared: "**O God you are my God; early will I seek you; my soul is thirsty for you, my flesh longs for you in a dry and thirsty land, where no water is.**" That verse tells me that God should be the focus of our daily lives not our desires and pursuits.

I do not want to grow complacent in my Christian life therefore I must continually seek Him and what He would have for me each day.

A.W. Tozer once said: *"**Complacency is a deadly foe. The desire daily for God must be present or there will be no manifestation of Christ to His people. He wants to be wanted by His people.**"* As I read that quote, I began to think about how important it is for me to keep Christ the focus of my life.

When you think about the challenges we have in raising our children, it is critical for us to realize that we can become complacent. We should be reminded as Tozer says that it could be devastating to our kids if we grow complacent in our approach to truth and our desire for an intimate relationship with God.

We should be determined more than ever that we do not want our lives in Christ to be something that we endure. We should want to live our lives in a way that pleases and honors God. I am afraid that so many people view God as part of their lives and not as the primary pursuit of their life.

I want more than ever to make a difference in the lives of my children. My desire is that we would always be distinctly Biblical in all that we do.

Not If but When

We will equally face many good and bad times in this lifetime. This is especially true when it comes to raising our children.

We are not called to be their friend or make decisions that are popular with them if we are committed to doing what is best for them. As well, we must recognize that they will make mistakes and fail. What will we do when that happens? Where will we stand during these moments? Will we throw the towel in and become discouraged?

It is easy sometimes to think that we as Christians should be immune to disappointments and discouraging events when we are not. I ran across a great quote that reads:

> *"Expecting the world to like you because you're a good person is like expecting the bull not to charge because you're a vegetarian."*
> *-anonymous*

The difference for Christians is that when we face difficulties we have hope because we are anchored in a relationship with an all-powerful God who can help us through any situation we may face. I want you to see two verses below that give us this hope:

> *Daniel 2:20-21: "Blessed be the name of God forever and ever: for wisdom and might are his; and he changes the times and the seasons; he removes kings and establishes up kings; he gives wisdom unto the wise, and knowledge to them that know understanding."*

> *1 Corinthians 4:20: "For the Kingdom of God is not in word, but in power."*

Daniel reminds us that all wisdom and power is his. He can change seasons, times, and kings so surely, He can help us with any difficulty we may face as a parent. Being a member of the Kingdom of God gives us access to real power. It is not like the person we all know who just runs off at the mouth about how powerful he is but can never back it up. I am grateful that we serve a God who can do anything.

I love great praise music and one of my favorites is "Our God is greater." There is one line in that song that I especially love. It says: "**Our God is greater, our God is stronger, and our God is higher than anyone else.**" This is a truth we must continually remind ourselves of.

God is omnipotent which literally means **"all powerful".** I do not know of another concept more critical for Christians living today than understanding and embracing this one. We will quickly be overwhelmed and discouraged in trying to raise our children without living out the idea that God alone is able to give us the power and wisdom we need for whatever task we may be facing.

So, how do we practically live out this concept? Ephesians 6:10 tells us to **"*be strong in the Lord and in the power of His might.*"** What does this mean? It means that in our mind and in our heart, we know and claim daily that He is all powerful. Specifically, we daily recognize that we cannot rely on our own strength to face the difficulties of life and instead we must rely on His strength.

It is a certainty that we will face difficulties in raising our children. It is not a matter of if but when and how often we will face them.

Three Ways to Protect Ourselves and Our Children from This Destructive Culture

"Don't copy the behavior and customs of this world, but let God transform you into a new person by changing the way you think. Then you will learn to know God's will for you, which is good and pleasing and perfect."
Romans 12:2

I am convinced that one of the dangers that we face today in Christianity is that of becoming too much like the world and not like Christ. The culture we live in is working hard to mold us and our children into its image. We see how this culture is using areas such as television and social media to attempt to transform our thinking. Even many churches today have abandoned elements of Biblical truth to be more cool and relevant to our culture.

How can we protect ourselves and our families from the effects of this culture and lead our families to be more like Christ? Romans 12:2 gives us three ways to do this.

1) <u>**We must not copy the customs and behavior of this culture.**</u>
Do others know that we are Christians by our lifestyle or do we simply fit into this culture?

2) <u>**We must allow Him to transform us.**</u>
Have we given our hearts completely to living for God and loving Him or is chasing the American dream our focus?

3) <u>**We need to allow God to change our thinking.**</u>
Has the world's definition of success kept us from God's design for our lives? Is modeling a Godly lifestyle for our children a priority for us? Do our kids see us studying God's Word? Do our kids see us pray? Better yet, do we pray with them?

Following the truth of Romans 12:2 will cause us to be looked upon differently by the world. Many will not understand this different way of thinking and will consider our path foolish. However, Romans 12:2 tells us that if we will do these three things then we will find God's will for our lives. Not only will we discover His will, but we will also discover a peace and contentment that God alone brings to our lives.

I read something Dr. Billy Graham said a few years back that illustrates the truth of Romans 12:2. Dr. Graham declared: ***"The men who followed Jesus were unique in their generation. They turned the world upside down because their hearts had been turned right side up. The world has never been the same."***

I pray that as we live out the truth of Romans 12:2 our world will never be the same!

Chapter 2
The Blessings of God

Convinced!

"Abraham never wavered in believing God's promise. In fact, his faith grew stronger, and in this he brought glory to God. He was fully convinced that God is able to do whatever he promises."
Romans 4:20-21

This summer my wife and I moved our youngest child into college. My daughter was understandably excited but also very nervous. She has always been a great student and hard worker but I could tell she was having some doubts and anxiety about doing college work. As I expected, she did great this past fall in school.

The truth is we all are confronted with doubts at times in our lives. The fear of the unknown can overwhelm us if we are not careful. In these times, I believe that we need to remind ourselves of what we can truly be convinced of in this life. God's Word gives us promises that we can not only hold onto but be convinced of their certainty. I want to share just a few promises today that you can be certain of.

1) <u>**God is with us as believers always**</u>
   We will never face a trial or difficulty alone. God has promised to be with us at all times to walk with us through the difficulties of life.
   Hebrews 13:5 "I will never leave thee, nor forsake thee."

2) <u>**God will finish in you what He started when He saved us**</u>
   God has a plan and purpose for our lives and we can trust Him to do in us what only He can do. ***Philippians 1:6 "And I am***

certain that God, who began the good work within you, will continue His work until it is finally finished on the day when Christ Jesus returns."

3) <u>God's love for us is everlasting</u>
We need to remember that there is nothing else we can do to make God love us anymore. *Jeremiah 31:3 "Long ago the LORD said to Israel: "I have loved you, my people, with an everlasting love. With unfailing love I have drawn you to myself."*

4) <u>God is faithful and His mercies are new everyday</u>
God is so faithful and each day He provides us with a new set of mercies to help us to face whatever may lie ahead. *Lamentations 3:23 "Great is His faithfulness; His mercies begin afresh each morning."*

5) <u>We are more than conquerors</u>
Romans 8:37 "in all these things we are more than conquerors through Him that loved us."

I pray that each of us will be convinced as Paul says in Romans 4:20-21 *"that God is able to do whatever He promises."* That is the kind of unwavering faith that I want for my life.

More Than Promises

"And because of his glory and excellence, he has given us great and precious promises. These are the promises that enable you to share his divine nature and escape the world's corruption caused by human desires."
2 Peter 1:4

There are times in all our lives that we have made promises that we have not kept. Most of those times we did not do so intentionally. We forgot many times or just got so overloaded that we just could not get it done. That is the human part of who we are.

I am so grateful that we serve a God who is not only perfect at keeping what He has promised but also giving us so much than we could ever imagine. 2 Peter 1:4 tells us that He has given ***"us great and precious promises."*** I love how the verse begins with the fact that we can access the promises because of who God's ***"glory and excellence."*** This verse goes on to tell us that these promises give us an enormous amount of power.

Peter describes this power when he tells us that we can ***"share His divine nature".*** What exactly does that mean? 1 Peter 1:23 describes it best when it declares:

> ***"For you have been born again, but not to a life that will quickly end. Your new life will last forever because it comes from the eternal, living word of God."***
> ***1 Peter 1:23***

We share His nature in that we as believers have eternal life. A life as that verse says will ***"last forever because it comes from the eternal, living word of God."*** What an incredible gift from God for this life!

More than that, Peter goes on to remind us that His promise is also to help us ***"escape the world's corruption."*** God promised to give us the power through His Holy Spirit to overcome sin, temptation, and corruption. How does He do that? Because ***"the Spirit who lives in you is greater than the spirit who lives in the world." 1 John 4:4***

Proverbs 29:6 also tells us that ***"Evil people are trapped by sin, but the righteous escape, shouting for joy."*** Praise the Lord we do not have to live trapped by sin or corruption. Christ because of His "glory and excellence" has set us free.

I know from my own life that this kind of freedom comes with joy, peace, and contentment for this life and security for the next life. I do not know what kind of trials you may be encountering today but I pray 2 Peter 1:4 will remind you today that God has made you promises as His child that He will keep, and these promises offer us so much more than we could have ever hoped for!

The Blessing of Recognizing Our Need for God

"There are two kinds of pride, both good and bad. 'Good pride' represents our dignity and self-respect. 'Bad pride' is the deadly sin of superiority that reeks of conceit and arrogance."
John C. Maxwell

When I look back at the history of our school, I am amazed at how God has blessed us and grown us in a short amount of time. If not careful, it would be easy to possibly get a little prideful at times thinking that we have arrived as a school. With that thought in mind, I have asked God to guard our hearts from any thoughts of this kind that represent the **"bad pride"** that John Maxwell mentions above.

We must always recognize that the only reason we have seen great things at MCA is because of God and not anything we did. MCA is a miracle of God's grace and work. As a school, we did not deserve anything we have been blessed with but God in His rich grace and mercy has seen fit to bless us.

It is so important that we realize that the same principle holds true in our daily walk with God. I love the **"Be Attitude"** mentioned in Matthew 5:3.

> *"God blesses those who are humble and realize their need for Him, for the Kingdom of Heaven is theirs."*

The truth of this verse is so powerful. It reminds us that ***"God blesses those who are humble and realize their need for Him."*** How does He do that? To begin with, He saved us when we recognized the need for Him. Next, He sanctifies or grows us in our spiritual walk when we give Him total control of our lives. In addition, God provides us with the ***"abundant life"*** He promised in John 10:10 when we recognize our need for Him. Most importantly, one day God will provide as Matthew 5:3 says the ***"Kingdom of Heaven"*** as our forever home!

The danger of not recognizing our daily need for God and thinking we know it all is to miss the greatest blessings that God has planned for us. I pray that the truth of Matthew 5:3 will speak to your heart and remind us all of God's great blessings. I leave you with the words of Paul in 1 Corinthians 2:9 that once again reiterate all that God has for us when we seek Him!

> *"That is what the Scriptures mean when they say, "No eye has seen, no ear has heard, and no mind has imagined what God has prepared for those who love him."*
> *1 Corinthians 2:9*

How to See God More Clearly

> *"God blesses those whose hearts are pure, for they will see God."*
> *Matthew 5:8*

A few years ago, I was driving through the mountains one night and I encountered a stretch of road where the conditions had turned terribly foggy. The fog was so thick that I had to slow down as I could only see a small portion of the road at a time. I struggled to see the road ahead and stay safe. I was anxious to see more clearly.

In a similar manner, many times we as Christians struggle to see where God wants to take us in our personal journey of life. Just like driving in fog, we are hard pressed to find our way as followers of Jesus. I am afraid that this process can become so intense that we too often default to the idea of just following our own desires rather than that of the Lord.

Matthew 5:8 gives us instead the inside information we need to see and experience God. The verse says that "God blesses those whose hearts are pure." What does all this mean and how do you experience the truth of this verse? I want to give you some things that I believe are essential to having a pure heart and seeing God.

1) <u>Having a pure heart means we must begin to live a life that is pleasing to God.</u>
   "What is more pleasing to the Lord: your burnt offerings and sacrifices or your obedience to his voice? Listen! Obedience is better than sacrifice, and submission is better than offering the fat of rams." 1 Samuel 15:22
   God has commanded us as believers to live by His truth. If we are to please God, we must obey His Word. Psalm 119:9 declares: **"How can a young man keep his way pure? By living according to your Word."** Are we devoted to His truth and living by that standard of truth? To see God more clearly, we must live by His Word!

2) <u>Having a pure heart also means that we must begin to live for the sole purpose of God.</u>
   A pure heart is evidenced by the way we live. 1 Peter 4:2 tells us that people devoted to God **"won't spend the rest of your lives chasing your own desires, but you will be anxious to do the will of God."** To see God more clearly, we must be

focused on chasing God's agenda for our lives rather than our own.

I do not know about you, but I no longer want to struggle to find my way in this life. Instead, I want to learn to live out the true meaning of Matthew 5:8. All the things that this world has to offer pales in comparison to truly seeing and experiencing God. Paul described this best in Philippians 3:7-8 when he said:

"I once thought these things were valuable, but now I consider them worthless because of what Christ has done. Yes, everything else is worthless when compared with the infinite value of knowing Christ Jesus my Lord."

Are You Ready to Rumble?

"God blesses those who work for peace, for they will be called the children of God."
Matthew 5:9

We live in a world that unfortunately loves to see a good fight. If you do not believe me, look no further than a lot of what is shown on reality television. Worldwide Wrestling may have created the phrase ***"Are you ready to rumble"*** but our society has adopted a lot of that philosophy.

How do I know this to be true? I see it unfortunately in how people will treat each other in the market place as we fight for what we believe to be our rights. I see it in how people respond to each other on social media. Even in the Christian community, Christians all too often seek to bash others rather than seek peace.

However, God has called us as followers of His to a different standard. Matthew 5:9 teaches us that God blesses those who work for peace. So, what did Jesus mean by peacemaker in verse 9? A working definition of a peacemaker is a person who is actively seeking to reconcile people to God and to one another.

According to that definition, a peacemaker is not something you see as often as we should. It is quite the distinction, per Matthew 5:9. This verse describes two great benefits to be a peacemaker. Those two benefits are:

1) <u>**You will be happier**</u>
   The word blesses or blessed in that verse means "happy." God promises joy and contentment to those who work for peace. When you work to reconcile people with each other and God, you will find joy and peace when broken relationships come together. You will find joy unexplainable when you lead others to Christ.

2) <u>**You will discover who you really are**</u>
   Verse 9 declares "that you will be called the children of God." There is no greater joy than knowing you are a child of God and living as a child of God. Jesus described Himself in Isaiah as the "Prince of Peace." Following Jesus completely means living our lives as peacemakers seeking to bring reconciliation to others and to God. That is the essence of who God designed us to be as His followers.

What about us? Are we peacemakers? When is the last time we helped reconcile someone to God? When is the last time we sought to make peace with someone we are upset with? A person can only work towards peace if he is at peace with himself.

I pray that we all find the peace that God has promised us and use that to become a peacemaker for God. May we begin to live by the words of Romans 12:18 which says:

> *"If it be possible, as much as depends on you, live peaceably with all men."*

Finding What We Are Searching For

> *"Blessed are they which do hunger and thirst after righteousness: for they shall be filled."*
> *Matthew 5:6*

I heard someone say once that the older they get the more that they think about the *"hereafter."* By hereafter, he went on to say that as he goes into other rooms looking for something he forgets what he came for and wonders what *"he is hereafter."*

Life is like that sometimes as we seem to be in search of what is truly significant. We have a longing for something and many times we are so restless. We try to fill these longings with things, experiences, accomplishments, and exploits but the longing remains.

The prophet Jeremiah described this problem well when he said we are trying to drink and be satisfied from broken cisterns or wells. In other words, from a source that will never satisfy. I love how C.S. Lewis spoke to this issue when he said:

> *"If I find in myself a desire which no experience in this world can satisfy, the most probable explanation is that I was made for another world."*

As C.S. Lewis said, we were indeed made for another world and thus our priorities ought to be different. Our focus as believers should be first and foremost to seek the Kingdom of Heaven.

Jesus gave the secret of being satisfied in Matthew 5:6. What did He mean by this verse? First, I think we need to recognize that Jesus is directing us to a new priority. To **"hunger and thirst after righteousness"** conveys the same meaning found in Matthew 6:33. That verse declares: **"But seek ye first the Kingdom of Heaven and His righteousness; and all these things will be added unto you."**

Can you imagine how our lives would change if we focused our lives around the idea of seeking God first? What would our days be like if we prioritized time with God each day before anything else? What would it be like if we sought God for what He would have us do with the decisions and directions of our lives?

The answer is found in Matthew 5:6. The last part of that verse tells us that we will be filled or satisfied. We will then begin to find what we are searching for!

Instead of pursuing all the things that this world can offer, we must recognize that the only way to find satisfaction in this life is to make Jesus Christ the #1 relationship of our lives and then pursue His agenda for our lives.

Many of you reading this today may be a little discouraged in your walk. My prayer is that God will use this verse to encourage each of us that He is the only answer to our hearts longings!

Chapter 3
God's Plan

A Plan That Will Work

"For God saved us and called us to live a holy life. He did this, not because we deserved it, but because that was His plan from before the beginning of time— to show us His grace through Christ Jesus."
2 Timothy 1:9

There was a television show several years ago, entitled "The A Team" which was made into a movie not too long ago. The leader of that team would regularly use the phrase: **"Don't you love it when a plan comes together?"** The same idea holds true in life when something you plan for comes to fruition.

We have often heard that God has a plan for our lives, but I am afraid that many times we do not live like we believe that. Instead of seeking and following God's plan for our life, we venture out on our own haphazardly seeking what we believe to be best for us. Too often, following our own plan creates a huge mess of our life.

What do we do when we find ourselves in a mess of our own making? Max Lucado answers that question when he declares:

"The meaning of life. The wasted years of life. The poor choices of life. God answers the mess of life with one word: grace."

As the old hymn says: **"Grace, grace, God's grace, grace that is greater than all our sin."** Indeed, grace is greater than any mess we have in our life. Most of us do not realize that grace was God's plan all along.

That is the message of 2 Timothy 1:9 above that tells us that God's plan from **"the beginning of time was to show us grace through Christ Jesus."** This verse reminds us that God gave us grace so that we could be saved and live differently.

I am convinced that God never meant for us to live defeated lives. God never meant for us to be without hope or direction for our lives. God's plan from the start was to show us grace so that we might enjoy life as He meant for us to enjoy it. He meant for us to have a love, a joy, a peace, and a contentment that only He can provide.

If you find yourself in a mess today, be encouraged that God's grace is greater than your situation. Please remember that God has a plan for your life that He prepared long ago that you might be saved and live differently.

Finally, never forget that **"His grace is sufficient for you."** His grace is the only plan that will provide all you will ever need!

We Are Supposed to Be Salty!

"Let your speech be always with grace, seasoned with salt, that ye may know how ye ought to answer every man."
Colossians 4:6

Nowadays, when a person is referred to as *"salty"*, it is not a good thing. Salty is an adjective used today to describe someone when they are angry or agitated. We experience a lot of folks who are somewhat *"salty"* in person, in emails, and on social media. In fact, many times we ourselves can become *"salty"* with others in those previously mentioned venues.

I do not know about you but when I get this way with others I am quickly reminded by the Spirit of God that this is not the way He would prefer for me to treat others. However, I do believe that God desires that we be *"salty"* with others but not the way the world defines the term.

God wants us instead to follow the truth of Colossians 4:6 above and ***"let our speech be always with grace, seasoned with salt."*** Why does Paul say that our speech needs to be seasoned with salt? What does salt do?

Salt has been used in the past for seasoning, a preservative, and a disinfectant. These three uses can have a tremendous impact on others if used in a Christ like manner with others through our speech. Let me provide an example of each.

1) <u>**As a seasoning in our speech**</u>
Do we use our words to bring the nature and heart of God to others? Jesus commanded us in Matthew to ***"be salt and light."*** We should be adding a divine flavor to our conversations. We should reflect the character of Christ in our conversations whether it be in person, email, or social media. Do we create a thirst for Christ in others with the way we communicate?

2) <u>**As a preservative in our speech**</u>
Salt was used in times past to preserve foods like meat to prevent decay. Are we using our speech and our written words to help stop the moral decay around us? Our culture is in trouble and we desperately need believers who will use their words to positively impact people for the Kingdom.

3) **<u>As a disinfectant in our speech</u>**
   Are we using our words to help clean up areas of conflict with others? What would happen if we would use our words to help bring healing and reconciliation to others? Think of the situations and relationships that God could use us to help clean up if we could follow the truth of Colossians 4:6.

We live in a time where we need Christians who know how ***"to answer every man"*** as God would have us. Can you imagine how God could use us as a school family if we would make the commitment for our speech to be ***"always with grace, seasoned with salt?"*** My prayer is that we all might begin today to impact others by being a Biblically ***"Salty"*** Christian!

Running with Purpose

"Don't you realize that in a race everyone runs, but only one person gets the prize? So run to win! All athletes are disciplined in their training. They do it to win a prize that will fade away, but we do it for an eternal prize. So I run with purpose in every step. I am not just shadowboxing."
1 Corinthians 9:24-26

A few years ago, I was diagnosed with Type 2 diabetes. My dad had suffered through this disease for years. As a result, I was determined to do all I could to fight the effects of this disease. I learned quickly how exercise would help and soon I began to take up running. When I was younger, running was not something that I had the least bit of interest in. However, things were different now in that I now had a purpose for running. That purpose was to help me feel better and fight the effects of diabetes.

My commitment to run has stayed very consistent over the years because of the intensity of my purpose. There have been times when I just did not want to do it but God has given me the strength to persevere and stay on purpose. I have even had the great pleasure to run in many 5k type events. You could say that I have run with purpose and not just for something to do.

The same thing should be said of our Christian lives. We should not just go to church, read our Bibles, or pray occasionally because that was the way we were brought up. God never intended for us to live our Christian lives in a mediocre fashion nor without purpose. Living for Jesus was never meant to be an exercise of just something to do.

Unfortunately, I am afraid that many have approached it as some tradition or something just to check off the list and not do it with a purpose. The results of such efforts are Christians who have a take it or leave it approach when it comes to going to church and spending time with God. Our world is full of Christians who sadly live without any power or purpose.

In 1 Corinthians 9:24-27, the Apostle Paul gives us the challenge to do just the opposite. Paul instructs us to run to win! He tells us to run with a purpose. I believe that purpose is to follow hard after God and find His purpose for our lives. I do know that one of His main purposes four lives is that we would learn to love Him with our entire heart, soul, and mind. In order to do this, we must discipline ourselves to do it with the entirety of our being or with purpose.

I ran across something George Washington said that best illustrates what I am saying. Washington declared:

> *"Make sure you are doing what God wants you to do--then do it with all your strength."*

Are you frustrated today in your Christian experience? Do you ever feel as if there could be more to the Christian life than you are experiencing now? I pray that we would all examine ourselves to see if we are just **"shadowboxing"** as Paul describes or if we are truly running after God with purpose. My heart's desire is that I would always run with the purpose of becoming exactly who God has called me to be!

Biblical Worldview

"The Word of God well understood and religiously obeyed is the shortest route to spiritual perfection. And we must not select a few favorite passages to the exclusion of others. Nothing less than a whole Bible can make a whole Christian."
– A.W. Tozier

God blessed my wife Karen and me with three beautiful daughters. Each one of my girls is so different and unique. One of the areas that they are different in is their approach to academics through the years.

All three have done well in school but have gone about this pursuit quite differently.

For example, our middle daughter Katie always made pretty good grades throughout secondary school but probably never worked as hard as she could have in the process. Upon arriving in college, she found the work to be quite challenging and demanding of more than what she was accustomed to doing. I will never forget one day during her sophomore year that she called me to give me her new stunning revelation about academics.

She said: *"Dad, I have figured out that it really does pay to study!"* My sarcastic response was: *"You think!"* In simple terms, what Katie learned about academics is that *"**learning the curriculum changes the outcome.**"*

Similarly, God tells us in His Word that knowing His truth will change our lives. Jesus told us in John 8:32 that ***"if you know the truth, the truth will set you free."*** Knowing the truth will set us free to live for Jesus and experience the Christian life as God designed for us to live it. I heard a preacher say once that God did not give us His Word to satisfy our curiosity but **to change our lives.**

The early church was devoted to Biblical teaching. They were committed to knowing the truth and allowing it to determine the direction of their lives. Acts 2:42 declares that *"**all of the believers**"* were devoted to Biblical teaching not just a few.

Research tells us today that only about 9% of all evangelicals have a Biblical worldview and as a result their ideas about sin and the absolutes of God's Word are quite contrary to Biblical teachings. This research tells us that they are not devoted to the truth of God's Word.

What is worldview? It is best defined as our underlying system of beliefs that shape our values and attitudes. Having a Biblical worldview means that we make all of the decisions of life through the lens of God's Word. Living with a Biblical worldview affects every area of our lives not just the church part.

How do we attain a Biblical Worldview? We attain a Biblical Worldview by being taught the truth of God's Word and also through personal study of the Bible. I pray that we would all stop and think about what we are allowing to shape our worldview. I pray that as Christians would search the Bible for all aspects of how to live this life so that we might be set free as Jesus promised.

Make Sure No One Misses Out

"See to it that no one misses the grace of God. And that no bitter root grows up to cause trouble and defile many."
Hebrews 12:15

The word *"grace"* is used a lot in Christian circles. I am afraid it is used so much that we have at times lost the significance of what it really means for our daily lives. Grace has been defined as **"the free and unmerited favor of God, as manifested in the salvation of sinners and the bestowal of blessings."**

That definition sounds good but what does it look like in real life?

1) <u>**Grace Provides Salvation**</u>
   Grace has often been described as God's riches at Christ's expense. In other words, Jesus gave His life on the cross as payment for our sins. It is His free and unmerited gift to us. Ephesians 2:8-9 describes it best when it says: **"For by grace are ye saved through faith; and that not of yourselves: it is the gift of God. Not of works, lest any man should boast."**

   I pray that we as Christians would never forget how great a gift that God has given us in salvation through His Son. When I think of the abundant life that I have been given in Christ, I want to make sure that I do all I can to make sure that others hear of His gift. I want to, as Hebrews 12:15 says above, "see to it that no one misses grace."

2) <u>**Grace Provides Power for Living**</u>
   The apostle Paul in 2 Corinthians 12:9-10 tells us: **"My grace is all you need. My power works best in weakness. So now I am glad to boast about my weaknesses, so that the power of Christ can work through me. That's why I take pleasure in my weaknesses, and in the insults, hardships,**

persecutions, and troubles that I suffer for Christ. For when I am weak, then I am strong."

I hope you do not miss the treasure found in these two verses. His grace is sufficient for all our needs. According to these verses, when we admit that we are weak and cannot solve the issues we are facing that is when God unleashes His grace and His power on our lives.

I know that to be true in my own life as I have personally experienced God's grace at my weakest and most desperate moments. Paul mentions some problems we all face in insults, hardships, and persecutions in these verses but also says that he can take pleasure in them because the grace of God is sufficient for meeting all those circumstances. What a promise from God that we need to claim!

Once again, I do not want anyone to miss out on *"**the grace of God"*** that can provide real lasting power for living this life. I pray that we would all begin to admit our weaknesses to God and allow Him to be strong on our behalf. When we do not have what it takes, God is telling us that He does!

For those of you who may be discouraged today, I pray that these verses will encourage your soul and remind us all that when we need strength the only place to find it is in the arms of the Lord!

Abundant Living

"I pray that from his glorious, unlimited resources he will empower you with inner strength through his Spirit. Then Christ will make his home in your hearts as you trust in him.

Your roots will grow down into God's love and keep you strong. And may you have the power to understand, as all God's people should, how wide, how long, how high, and how deep his love is. May you experience the love of Christ, though it is too great to understand fully. Then you will be made complete with all the fullness of life and power that comes from God."
Ephesians 3:16-19

Most people are in search of the good life. Unfortunately, most people search in all the wrong places for it. The resources provided by this world will never satisfy and can be easily lost. I love the rich passage found in Ephesians 3:17-18. This passage provides us with a clear guide to finding the abundant life. Let me share with you the treasures of this passage.

1) <u>**God Alone is the Only Sustainable Source of Strength for this Life**</u>
   Verse 16 above tells us that God's resources are not only unlimited and glorious but capable of giving us the inner strength we need for this life.

2) <u>**God's Love Can Keep You Strong**</u>
   If we will trust Him, He promises in verse 17 to **"make His home in our hearts."** Abundant living begins with developing a real love relationship with God and allowing our roots to **"grow down into God's love."** When we do this, He promises to keep us strong no matter what we encounter in this life.

3) <u>**Gaining an Understanding of God's Love Will Change Your Life**</u>
   Verse 18 challenges us to pray for and seek a true understanding of God's love for us. We see this understanding as we study God's Word. In Deuteronomy 32:10, He calls us the **"apple of His eye."** God calls us His **"beloved"** in Deuteronomy 33:12 and Romans 9:25. Song of Solomon 2:4 says His **"banner over**

us is love." Romans 8:38 tells us that *"nothing can separate us from God's love."* If we could begin to grasp His love for us it would change our perspective, our outlook, and our life.

4) <u>**We Have an Opportunity to Have More Than We Could Ever Dream Possible**</u>
Verse 19 is expressing Paul's desire that we *"may experience the love of Christ."* If we can experience that love, Paul tells us that then we can truly find the abundant life that God promised.

Webster defines abundant as *"marked by great plenty."* The abundant life God promises is not the same plenty as the world promises. Instead, God offers us peace, joy, contentment, meaning, purpose, and His power for living at our disposal. How much more could we ask for?

What Do You See?

"Be still, and know that I am God! I will be honored by every nation. I will be honored throughout the world."
Psalm 46:10

I have never been one who likes to sit still. Growing up, it was quite a challenge to get me to sit and do my work in school. Even as an adult, I have had to work at relaxing and allowing myself not to feel compelled to get up and do something. The idea of just sitting still is an issue many people struggle with in life.

This is especially true when it comes to our spiritual wellbeing. We turn to so many other things in life for answers and direction other than the Lord. When an issue in life arises, many times Christians are eager to go solve it by turning to others, ourselves, or the things of this world.

Turning to these other things for answers is like putting sunscreen on a broken arm. It really does not address our deepest need.

Psalm 46:10 gives us a new approach to dealing with the issues of life. He tells us that we need to stop going to these other sources for help first and instead give our full attention deliberately to the living Lord. In his words, to sit there and be still knowing that He is God.

What does it look like to **"be still and know that I am God?"** I believe it means to focus on worshipping Him, meditating on Him, and pouring through His word for what He would say to us. I believe that our focus would change if we would stop and reflect on His grace, His mercy, His love, His power, and His might rather than our present circumstances.

When we are focused on life's circumstances, it prohibits us from really seeing what the Lord would have us to see. When we focus only on our circumstances, too often we only see insurmountable obstacles rather than a God who is more powerful than any of that.

This was true in the Old Testament when the Israelite spies were sent by Moses to scout out the Promised Land. Most of the spies came back seeing only giants and an impenetrable fortress. But Caleb and Joshua had their eyes fixed on something else. They saw the promises of God, the truth of His Word, and that He could overcome all of that.

What do you see today? Are you overwhelmed by problems that seem so impossible to deal with? I hope that we would all be reminded by Psalm 46:10 to **"be still and know that He is God."** Doing this would enable us to see that He is bigger than anything we are facing today.

I pray that this verse will not only encourage your heart today but also give us all the impetus to seek God first in our approach to everything we will face in this life!

Someone You Can Count On

**"Then Elijah stood in front of them and said, "How much longer will you waver, hobbling between two opinions?"
1 Kings 18:21**

We all have those moments in life when we are faced with what seems to be a difficult choice to make. In making those choices, what should we rely on to make the right choice? The far safer choice is to choose the option that has the best possibility of an outcome with some element of certainty. Most people are more likely to go with something or someone that you can count on in a pinch.

This is essentially the same situation that the prophet Elijah spoke about in 1 Kings 18 when he challenged the people of Israel to make a choice about who they were going to serve. He is asking them why they are vacillating between the one true God and other substitutes who have no real power.

If not careful, we can spend our lives chasing things that have no real power to satisfy our soul. The urgency of our jobs and the desire to chase the American dream can have us wavering as Elijah described. The things of this world will never be what we need in times of difficulty and crisis when we need someone or something to count on.

The truth is that most of life is lived in the valley and not on the mountain top. In the valley, we quickly discover that wavering in our faith is of no comfort. During those times, we find peace and comfort in serving the one true God. All of this begs the question then of why we do not just make serving God the priority of our lives.

Why not trust Him in both the good times and the bad times? Why waver on a God who can be trusted? I love how Deuteronomy 7:9 describes how faithful God is to those who choose to love and follow Him.

"Understand, therefore, that the Lord your God is indeed God. He is the faithful God who keeps His covenant for a thousand generations and lavishes His unfailing love on those who love Him and obey His commands."

We all need someone to count on in this life. There is just no need to vacillate any longer. I pray that we will boldly step out in faith and trust and serve God with every bit of our lives. As Deuteronomy 7:9 says, He is a God who keeps His Word and "lavishes His unfailing love on us."

What more could we ask for than to serve a God we can trust and one who loves us unconditionally?

Chapter 4
What Matters!

What Really Matters!

"I pray that your love will overflow more and more, and that you will keep on growing in knowledge and understanding. For I want you to understand what really matters, so that you may live pure and blameless lives until the day of Christ's return."
Philippians 1:9-10

We live in the most digitally connected culture of all time. We have access to more information and knowledge than at any other time in history. However, I am afraid that we spend more time with technology screens than with anyone else. Research tells us that the average American spends anywhere from 7 to 10 hours a day in front of a screen of some sort.

It seems as if there is no place in our lives that is void of a technological device. Our culture spends more time engaging with technology, social media, and entertainment than with each other.

In Philippians 1:9-10, Paul is admonishing us to grow **"in knowledge and understanding"** so that we will understand what matters. We all need to stop and ask ourselves what is most important to us. Is it all that important that we keep up with the latest on what is happening on social media or engage our children in conversation at dinner? Do we spend more time on Facebook and Twitter than we do in God's Word?

Paul says above that the goal is ***"to understand what really matters, so that you can live pure and blameless lives."*** I believe that most Christians desire to have this kind of life for themselves and their children. So, how do we go about putting some controls back in our lives in this technological age so that we can accomplish this goal?

To begin with, we must establish some hard and fast priorities for our families that cannot be compromised. Below are some examples of these type priorities:

1) **<u>Set aside time with your family each day to discuss the things of God</u>**
   If we are going to grow in understanding, we must spend time in God's Word each day ourselves and spend time discussing it with our children.

2) **<u>Set the priority that Sunday is the day you go to church</u>**
   "I was glad when they said unto me, Let us go into the house of the Lord." Psalm 122:1 There is no better way to disconnect from this world and grow together in knowledge and understanding than to go to church as a family. Are you glad when it is church time or have we given the priority of that day away to things that really do not matter?

3) **<u>Set aside times and places where we do not use devices</u>**
   A great way to focus on what matters and build relationships within the family is to have time and places where you put away devices. The dinner table is a great place to start as it is time where we can engage our families and has been shown by research to be an effective way to build a healthy family. Another great place to forbid devices is in the bedrooms of our houses. Children do not need unfettered access to the internet in an unprotected area. Another great place to forbid devices is in the car as you can have great conversations on the way to places with a captive audience.

God desires to enrich our lives with the things that matter! I pray that the truth of Philippians 1:9-10 will remind us to seek those things and not what this world offers!

Standing for What Really Matters

"In matters of style, swim with the current; in matters of principle, stand like a rock."
– Thomas Jefferson

It is fascinating to watch styles come and go over the years. Whether it be hair styles or clothing, it seems that styles go in cycles. I will never forget the leisure suits of the 1970's and their unusual style. I pray that this is one style that would never make a comeback.

Style do come and go and most times hold no real significance to the meaning of life. As a follower of Jesus, I instead want to focus my attention on things that do matter in this life. I love to study the life of Daniel in the Old Testament. Daniel lived in a very tough culture that was constantly trying to remake him to be like them instead of who God designed him to be.

Much like Daniel, we live in a culture that is trying to take us in a direction that is anything but holy. This is a culture where Christianity is not celebrated but instead ridiculed. Daniel approached his day with strength and resolve. In fact, Daniel 11:32 says:

"But the people who know their God will be strong and take action."

Daniel's approach in this verse is one we should emulate today. I want to share with you two key truths from this verse. First, we need to be reminded that there is strength in the Lord. Nehemiah 8:10 specifically reminds us of this when it declares:

> ***Don't be dejected and sad, for the joy
> of the Lord is your strength!"***

We can be strong. We can be strong and passionate in our convictions, our decisions, and our beliefs if they are consistent with God's truth. But, we should also know there are going to be times that we will suffer for it. 2 Thessalonians 3:12 tells us:

> ***"Yes, and everyone who wants to live a godly life
> in Christ Jesus will suffer persecution."***

Finally, the second part of Daniel 11:32 tells us to act. We ought to be focused on making a difference for Christ in this difficult culture. I think as we are standing strong in the strength of the Lord we should also be loving in our approach. We ought to be more focused than ever before in sharing the Gospel with hurting world. We ought to be more determined than ever before to help those who are hurting and showing them tangibly the love of God. We ought to lovingly stand for what we believe in without destroying those who disagree with us.

That is exactly the approach Daniel used in his day. I pray that we will as Christians "be strong and take action" in ways that will glorify our great God!

The Secret to Long Life

> *"The quality, not the longevity, of one's
> life is what is important."*
> Martin Luther King, Jr.

Since the days of Ponce de Leon's search for the fountain of youth, our world has been looking for ways to live longer and put off death. You can see this by simply watching the commercials and see all the medications, diets, exercise plans, and more being advertised that will help not only prolong life but make us feel better and younger.

I do believe that taking care of ourselves and striving for a healthy lifestyle is something God would have us to do. However, I also believe that God's Word goes beyond these ideas to present us with what it means to live a true life of quality. Proverbs 22:4 gives us great insight into what quality living looks like from a Biblical standpoint.

> *"True humility and fear of the* Lord *lead to riches, honor, and long life."*

Solomon provides us in this verse with two things that should serve as our focus for living. First, he talks of living with *"true humility."* Our world is consumed with taking selfies which underscores the real issue of this age. That issue is a society that is dominated by a concern for self. Solomon is telling us just the opposite. He is instructing us that life should not be about us but instead a true humility.

What is a true humility? I believe it is an attitude as Paul said in Philippians that *"esteems others more than yourself."* It is a lifestyle that is characterized by Galatians 2:20 that says, *"Not I but Christ."*

The second thing we are to focus on is fear of the Lord. What is the fear of the Lord? It is an awe and reverence of God that we should build our lives upon. Proverbs 9:10 tells us:

> *"Fear of the* Lord *is the foundation of wisdom."*

A fear of the Lord will compel us to allow God to be the preeminent or most important relationship of our lives. With that in place, we will then begin to make our everyday decisions in a way that seeks to honor Him and not promote us. It is *"foundation of wisdom"* to build our lives upon.

Solomon not only gives us these two keys, but he seals it by giving us the result of following these strategies. He declares that it will **"lead to riches, honor, and long life."** Not riches as the world would describe but a rich lifestyle that only God can provide. A life that would be marked by peace, joy, contentment, self-control, and more.

Also, it produces honor. This type of lifestyle will do as Luke 2:52 says and give us "favor with God and favor with man." No greater way to be remembered than as someone who has lived honorable before the Lord.

Finally, Proverbs 22:4 tells us that pursuit of these two things will lead to long life. The real secret is that if we will focus on the quality of life as God prescribes and not the longevity of it is that God stands ready to give us so much more.

Chapter 5
Distinctive Living

How to Speak in a Way That Will Be Heard

"Let no corrupt communication proceed out of your mouth, but that which is good to the use of edifying, that it may minister grace unto the hearers."
Ephesians 4:29

I walked through our school office last year and observed two prospective students texting while sitting in our lobby and when I stopped to introduce myself I also humorously asked one who they were texting. To my surprise, he pointed to the student on the other side of the lobby. With all the technology that we have today, I am not sure that communication has really improved.

George Bernard Shaw once quipped: **"The single biggest problem in communication is the illusion that it has taken place."** I think that statement still holds true today in many cases. However, miscommunication may be an even bigger problem than the lack of communication that exists. I see this so often when I observe all that goes on in social media posts.

It grieves my heart to see so many of the unhealthy posts that appear on social media. It is bothersome to see people post negative comments or thoughts about someone else or to agree with someone who is doing that. I heard someone say once that *"you are what you post."* I am afraid that could become what our testimony looks like to those around us if we do not take a different approach.

As Christians, I am convinced that God does hold us to a higher standard. Ephesians 4:29 is clear in telling us what kind of communication should come out from us. If we follow the truth of this verse, we can begin to communicate in a way that we can be assured that we will be heard.

First, we need to make sure that we do not allow anything unwholesome or harmful to come out of our mouth or in anything we post. I understand that we all get upset about certain situations and we want to be heard. However, this verse does not give us that option. It says **"no corrupt communication"** and does not give an exception when we feel we have been wronged in some way. If we will speak the truth in love, we can begin to be heard.

Next, we are to use words that will edify others. What does it mean to edify? In the Christian context, it means to strengthen someone or be strengthened in relationship to God, the Christian walk, and holiness. We cannot say or post negative things about someone else and expect to edify at the same time. If we want to be heard, we must look to edify others.

Finally, we want to minister grace to the people who will hear what we have to say. How is grace defined? **"Grace may be defined as the unmerited or undeserving favor of God".** Ephesians 4:29 is calling us to minister that same kind of unmerited favor to others when they speak. How do we do that? We do that by showing respect and honor to others in how we speak or post. We also do that by going directly to that person and not to others to talk about whatever the issue is. If we want to be heard, we must minister grace to others.

I want to be the kind of Christian who follows the truth of Ephesians 4:29. I pray that I will always communicate this way with others. As well, I pray that you will always do the same for us. In doing so, I believe that God will be glorified, and our relationships will grow stronger.

A Needed Mind Set

"Don't be selfish; don't try to impress others. Be humble, thinking of others as better than yourselves. Don't look out only for your own interests, but take an interest in others, too."
Philippians 2:3-4

My family went to Disney this past summer and as usual the crowds were enormous, and it was incredibly hot. In that environment, it seems as if everyone is working so hard to be ahead of others. We do not like to wait, and we especially do not like it if we feel someone has jumped ahead of us wrongfully. If we are not careful a "me first" mindset can overtake us at times. We live in such a fast-paced world that this mindset often wins the day.

Not only are we in a hurry but there is a great desire within human nature to want to impress others and be recognized. A big danger is that we can even begin to think we are better than others.

The type of thinking described above runs so contrary to the mindset God desires for each of us to possess. God desires that we instead pursue living our lives with the **"mind of Christ."** What is the mind of Christ? Philippians 2:5-8 describes the mind of Christ.

"Let this mind be in you, which was also in Christ Jesus: Who, being in the form of God, thought it not robbery to be equal with God: But made Himself of no reputation, and took upon Him the form of a servant, and was made in the likeness of men: And being found in fashion as a man, He humbled Himself, and became obedient unto death, even the death of the cross."

The mind of Christ was about giving His life for us so that we might have not only eternal life but an abundant life here on earth. This passage tells us that He **"humbled Himself."** In Philippians 2:3-4 above, Paul admonished us to do the same. Paul is instructing us to be humble and to think of others before ourselves.

The world desperately needs to see Christians with this kind of mindset. For way too long, the church has been known for what it is against and I think it is time for us to become known more for what we are for. I am convinced we should show the world that we are for loving and helping others. We must begin to look out and care for others before we think of ourselves. Talk about a radical lifestyle and mindset!

I leave you with a quote that asks us all a very important question about our mindset.

> *"Life's most persistent and urgent question is, 'What are you doing for others?'"*
> **Dr. Martin Luther King, Jr.**

May God move on our hearts daily to love,
care, and meet the needs of others!

Who Are You Going to Trust?

> *"It's hard to hear from God when you have your mind made up."*
> **Dr. Mike Whitson**

I am sure most of us have heard someone say of another that they have **"trust issues."** The meaning being that this person has developed a hard time trusting other. I am afraid sometimes as Christians we develop the same problem when it comes to trusting God completely. We have problems and difficulties come our way and many times we instinctively choose to find our plan for dealing with the problem and never taking it to God.

I wonder how often we make our minds up about something without spending time in prayer or God's Word to see if our solution lines up with what God has to say. In my life, I have been guilty of doing this so many times. You would think that with all the mistakes I have made doing it this way that I would have learned that not choosing to trust God is never the best option.

On the other hand, I have found God to be so faithful over the years and worthy of me trusting Him with every aspect of my life. Years ago, I found Him faithful and trustworthy in leading me to my wife. At first, I tried to find someone on my own and that proved to be very unfruitful. When I turned that process over to God and trusted Him with the results, God led me to the greatest gift of my life outside of salvation in my wife.

When I became a father, I struggled with how to raise my children and leaned heavily on my own wisdom. This too proved to be so frustrating and I quickly learned that being a parent was all about following God's plan completely and trusting Him with the results. From that experience, God did miraculous things with my kids and has grown them up to be intimate followers of Jesus Christ. He has given me joy through their lives and walk that I would have never experienced had I continued to raise them on my own.

Over and over in my life God has proved so faithful and trustworthy. Yet, there are times that we all wander back to the idea of trusting ourselves or someone else in day to day aspects of life. I am convinced that if we would all as believers when faced with a decision or crisis take a step back and consider all the times in our lives when God has shown Himself so strong and trustworthy in our lives then I am sure we would choose more often to trust God.

The Apostle Paul in 1 Corinthians 2:5 conveys this idea when he says: ***"I did this so you would trust not in human wisdom but in the power of God."*** Paul is telling the church at Corinth that he has modeled for them the principle of completely trusting God and relying on His power alone so that they too might learn to trust in the power of God.

I pray that we all would learn to seek God first with the details of our everyday lives and keep our minds and hearts open to the voice of God so that we might hear daily what He has to say to us. God does have great things planned for our lives if we will learn to trust Him!

Submission

One of the most misunderstood aspects of discipleship is that of submission. People have all kinds of wrong ideas about submission especially when it comes to areas such as marriage. What does it mean?

Submission means willingly choosing to let someone else lead. It is an act of choice made to prepare the believer for his own submission to God.

The Bible is full of admonition for believers in the area of submission. Let's look at few that theologian Richard Foster has given:

1) <u>Submission to God</u>
   "We must obey God rather than man." Acts 5:29. We must learn to submit our lives and obey God.

2) <u>Submission to scripture</u>
   "All Scripture is inspired by God and profitable for teaching, for reproof, for correction, for training in righteousness." 1 Timothy 3:17 We must learn to live under the authority of God's Word.

3) <u>Submission to our family</u>

"Do not merely look out for your own interests, but also for the interests of others." Philippians 2:4. We must consider others before ourselves. I have learned as the man of the house that I am to love my wife as Christ loved the church. How did He do that? He gave Himself sacrificially for the church. I am to love my wife and children sacrificially.

4) <u>Submission to our neighbors</u>
"Do nothing from selfishness or empty conceit, but with humility of mind regard one another as more important than yourselves." Philippians 2:3 Again, we must consider others before ourselves. Life is not about us or our rights.

5) <u>Submission to the body of Christ</u>
"Obey your leaders, and submit to them; for they keep watch over your souls, as those who will give an account. Let them do this with joy and not with grief, for this would be unprofitable for you." Hebrews 13:17

6) <u>Submission to the broken, the despised</u>
"Pure and undefiled religion in the sight of our God and Father is this, to visit orphans and widows in their distress, and to keep oneself unstained by the world." James 1:27
We need to be about helping those who need our help and sharing the love of Christ with them.

7) <u>Submission to the world</u>
"For God so loved the world that He gave His only begotten Son that whosoever believed on Him might be saved." John 3:16. I have been taught so well the idea that we are never more like God than when we give. God gave His only Jesus so that we might have the forgiveness of sin and eternal life. We need to be about submitting our lives sharing the Good News of Jesus Christ to others.

Submission is not an ugly word nor is it something we should avoid. Submission is a spiritual discipline we all need so that we may daily more experience the life and joy that God has for us.

We Do Not Have to Be Mean

"Never water down the Word of God, preach it in its undiluted sternness; there must be unflinching loyalty to the Word of God, but when you come to personal dealing with your fellow men, remember who you are- not a special being made up in Heaven, but a sinner saved by grace."
Oswald Chambers

We live in a day where there is plenty of division in our world. The division has become so great at times that we see violence as a result. Christianity is under attack in this culture. Our core beliefs are regularly mocked and derided. The question for us as believers is how we should respond.

I am sad to say that far too often Christians have responded in hateful and destructive ways which I believe further hurt our cause. At times, Christians have been mean. I agree with Oswald Chambers above that we should be committed to the Word of God without compromise. But also, we should as he says remember that we are just **"a sinner saved by grace."**

The people that attack Christians and Christianity are not our enemy. Ephesians 6:12 confirms this when it says:

"For we are not fighting against flesh-and-blood enemies, but against evil rulers and authorities of the unseen world, against mighty powers in this dark world, and against evil spirits in the heavenly places."

Ephesians 6:12

Our battle is not against man. It would do us well to remember that God loves them as much as He loves us and that it would take no more grace to save them as it did us. Therefore, we must engage this culture with a very balanced approach.

We must stand for truth but do so in the love of Christ. I love the way Paul described it in Ephesians 4:15 when he declared:

> ***"Instead, we will speak the truth in love, growing in every way more and more like Christ, who is the head of his body, the church."***
> ***Ephesians 4:15***

Jesus was confronted, assaulted, and crucified by the culture of His day and yet He ***"spoke the truth in love."*** This is my prayer for my life that I would stand for truth without compromise but while doing so that I would love people. What does this look like?

It means respecting the rights of others to have a different opinion and loving them regardless while we share what we believe is God's truth. We do not have to be mean. We are to stand for truth. May we begin to pray the truth of 2 Peter 1:2 that declares:

> ***"May God give you more and more grace and peace as you grow in your knowledge of God and Jesus our Lord."***
> ***2 Peter 1:2***

Impossible to Overlook

Our culture has worked so hard in recent years to do everything possible to remove God from all aspects of the public square. This has systematically been going on for many years in our country. God has been left out and ignored in much of our culture.

For Christians, this is difficult because we believe that God is created everything, and His fingerprints are on every aspect of this world. So, how could we possibly leave Him out? However, many times we as Christians leave Him out of our decision making and planning choosing to rely on our wisdom rather than His. I know this to be true because I have relied on my own wisdom far too many times instead of depending on God's wisdom.

Paul in Colossians 2:3 tells us:

"In him lie hidden all the treasures of wisdom and knowledge."
Colossians 2:3

This verse reminds us that in God alone we will find all wisdom and knowledge. His wisdom far surpasses anything we can imagine on our own. We cannot leave Him out and expect to have what we need to live this life victoriously.

Even more, this verse reminds us of the importance of Christian Education. Here at MCA, we do not leave God out of anything. We believe that God has something to say about everything in life including subject areas such as math, science, history, language, and all aspects of human behavior. A student cannot be totally prepared for this life without gaining a worldview that knows how to access God's "treasures of wisdom and knowledge"

We all have times in our lives where we struggle for answers to some of life's biggest problems. The answers we need are found in the hope and truth of God's Word. These treasures are not hidden or beyond our reach. They are available to us daily. For those of you who may be going through a difficult time finding the wisdom you need, I pray Colossians 2:3 will encourage you.

I also want to leave you with another verse of incredible promise for us as live. This great promise is described so well in 2 Peter 1:3 when Paul declares:

> *"By his divine power, God has given us everything we need for living a godly life. We have received all of this by coming to know him, the one who called us to himself by means of his marvelous glory and excellence."*

Indeed, God has given us everything we need to live this life and find peace, joy, and contentment. In His power, may we claim it daily!

Is Getting What We Want Always Best?

> *"If I would have given people what they wanted I would have given them a faster horse."*
> *– Henry Ford*

I remember as a kid growing up having all these things in mind that I wanted to have or to do when I became an adult. Like most kids, I wanted to be famous and have money. In fact, I wanted to be a pro football quarterback. As I got to junior high school, I decided to try and follow that dream by playing on the junior high football team. I knew that playing football was what I really wanted to do. It would satisfy my innermost longings.

In those days, I was so skinny that I had to run around in the shower to get wet and that lack of weight and strength did not bode well for me in football. Quickly into the season I realized that I did not like to get hit that much and soon thereafter I broke an arm which ended my season. At a very young age, I began to realize that I what I wanted at times was not always best for me.

This same principle holds true for us spiritually. We all have ideas of what we want out of this life and so often we are disappointed when fulfilling our wants does not satisfy our souls. Jesus offered an alternative in Matthew 6:33 for finding satisfaction and significance for our lives when He declared:

> ***"Seek the Kingdom of God above all else, and live righteously, and He will give you everything you need."***
> ***Matthew 6:33***

This verse reminds us that if we prioritize our relationship with God above all else and seek His desires for our lives then He will satisfy our longings and bring significance to our lives. We have this idea in our minds that if we follow God then we will lose out in life on what is best.

That type of thinking runs contrary to God's Word. Instead, God desires according to Paul in Ephesians 3:20 "***to do exceeding abundantly above all that we ask or think.***" God wants to do so much more than we could ever imagine with our lives if we will relinquish control. I love how the late missionary Jim Elliot described this principle when he said: ***"God always gives His best to those who leave the choice with Him."***

I have seen the truth of this principle in my own life. God has given me much more than I deserved or could have imagined when I have sought Him completely. He is a good, good Father who wants to do so much for us if we will just give our lives to Him. Psalm 37:4 embodies this truth: ***"Take delight in the L***ORD***, and he will give you your heart's desires."***

Don't You Just Love Do-Overs?

"Great is his faithfulness; his mercies
begin afresh each morning."
Lamentations 3:23

If you are like me, there are a lot of things or events in life that we wish we could do over. We believe in our heart of hearts that we will do better if we were given the chance. In a casual round of golf, you can take a mulligan or an opportunity to hit again if you hit a bad shot. Wouldn't it be great if we could get a mulligan for things in life we want to do better?

The good news is that God gives us something better each day of our lives. Lamentations 3:23 tells us because of God's great faithfulness we receive new mercies from Him every day. Each day, God delivers a new set of mercy to our lives. He is faithful and does not miss a day.

1 John 1:9 tells us that "If we confess our sins, He is faithful and just to forgive us." God stands ready each day to wipe our slate clean and fellowship with us in an intimate personal relationship. People will normally start over and make resolutions at the beginning of each year, but God gives us that opportunity every day.

As humans, we are going to fail and make mistakes, but God is so faithful to pick us up each time we fall. Beyond failing, we are also unfaithful at times in so many areas of our life but He never is unfaithful. I love Psalm 115:1 and how it describes this.

"Not to us, O Lord, not to us, but to your name goes all the glory for your unfailing love and faithfulness."

I am sure that there are some who are reading this who are very discouraged about how things may be going right now. I pray that Lamentations 3:23 will encourage your heart. I pray that it will remind you that we serve a merciful and loving God who wants to give you the mercy you need for whatever you are facing today!

Let's give Him all the glory as Psalm 115:1 says for His "unfailing love and faithfulness."

Happy

"The Constitution only gives people the right to pursue happiness. You have to catch it yourself."
Benjamin Franklin

Pharrell Williams recently recorded a song called "Happy" that has gone to the top of the charts here in America. The title and message of the song is great marketing because the idea of being happy clearly appeals to people of all ages. People throughout history have searched and sought for the key to being happy.

People have searched for fame, money, success, relationships, and so much more. When I was serving as a Singles' Minister at my church, I remember the number of people who would tell me that if they could just find someone to marry then they knew they would be happy. Not to be a wet blanket, but I would tell them finding happiness in that way will only make two people miserable. Instead, my advice to them was to first find peace, contentment, joy, significance, and happiness for yourself in a relationship with Jesus Christ. Only then, will you truly be content.

I love the "be attitudes" in Matthew chapter 5 where Jesus gives us some counter-cultural advice for how to live this life. The attitudes He describes in this chapter are not attitudes that you see regularly in our culture, but they are attitudes that I believe will bring peace, joy, contentment, significance, and even happiness to our lives.

One of those attitudes in verse 8 of that chapter really speaks to this issue. That verse says: "Blessed are the pure in heart: for they shall see God." The word blessed in this verse and the other be attitude verses literally means "happy." What does it mean when it says "happy are the pure in heart; for they shall see God?"

I am convinced that this verse is telling us that when we commit our lives and our hearts completely to God we will sense the peace, the joy, the contentment, the significance, and the happiness that only God can give and only God can sustain. When we live with an undivided heart towards God, we will be able to live with the assurance that whatever we face in this life is only temporary and that God has secured for us our eternity.

I pray that all of us will give hearts lavishly to the Lord Jesus so that we can experience the truth of Matthew 5:8.

Hold Nothing Back

The fear of losing someone or something very important to us will cause us to take some extra precautions. Many times, we will hold back and protect those people or things we are afraid of getting hurt. I am very protective of my three girls and I will do anything to keep them from getting hurt. There have been times in the past when I have taken extra precautions to check a situation out before I let them be a part of it to ensure their safety. Most parents would do this for the good of their children.

There are times when holding back is not such a good thing. At times, I am afraid that we hold back from giving God our entire love and devotion because other people or the lure of things have divided our hearts and have taken God's rightful place in our lives. There was a time in Abraham's life when God wanted Abraham to know that he loved God more than anything else and that he would not hold back anything from God.

That time came at Mt. Moriah when God asked Abraham to sacrifice his one and only son Isaac. Abraham loved God so much that he had laid his son on the altar and raised the knife to kill Isaac when God said in Genesis 22:12:

> *"Don't lay a hand on the boy!" the angel said. "Do not hurt him in any way, for now I know that you truly fear God. You have not withheld from me even your son, your only son."*

God saw a true fear for God in Abraham's life at that moment. God knew how Abraham would respond but I believe He wanted Abraham to see it and experience it. What does it mean to fear God as the passage says?

I believe it means a love, an awe, a respect, and a worship of God above anything else in this life. In the passage, God goes on to say that you have not withheld even your most prized possession from me. Abraham was demonstrating at Mt. Moriah that there was nothing in his life that he valued more than his relationship with God.

A true fear of God goes beyond just the big things of life but also encompasses obeying God in the little things of life. I love a quote by D.L. Moody that I ran across awhile back that speaks to this issue.

> *"There are many of us that are willing to do great things for the Lord, but few of us are willing to do little things."*

What about us? What are we holding back from God? Are we doing the little things in life each day to show that we value our relationship with God over anything else? Do we truly fear God? If we do, then we will have a heart like Abraham. That kind of heart says: "Lord, you are worthy above all else in my life and I hold nothing back from you."

I want to live a life that holds nothing back from God. I want to run hard after God the rest of my life. I want a heart that fears God and serves Him above all else.

Chapter 6
Difficult Times

How to Respond in Difficult Times

"And all things are of God, who hath reconciled us to Himself by Jesus Christ, and hath given to us the ministry of reconciliation; To wit, that God was in Christ, reconciling the world unto Himself, not imputing their trespasses unto them; and hath committed unto us the word of reconciliation."
2 Corinthians 5:18-19

We have witnessed over the years some very difficult times in our country. There are so many people who are hurting and heartbroken. There is also a lot of division in our country between people. How should the people of God respond? What should be the ministry of the church during these difficult times?

I have heard it said that sometimes our differences are irreconcilable. 2 Corinthians 5:18-19 reminds us that God is bigger than any difference that may exist. This passage reminds us that God bridged the greatest irreconcilable difference that ever existed when He sent Jesus to die on a cross for our sins. Our sins had separated us from God and created what seemed to be an irreconcilable difference. 2 Corinthians 5:18 tells us that God in His love and mercy overcame that difference and reconciled us to Jesus.

Now that we have been reconciled to Jesus, this passage tells us that we now have been given the ***"ministry of reconciliation."*** What does that type of ministry really look like? I believe that God is calling us to love others as we have never loved before. I believe He wants us to love others as He loved people. How does God love? Let me provide three characteristics of God's love. First, I believe He loved us sacrificially. John 3:16 tells:

> ***"For God so loved the world that He gave His only begotten Son, that whosoever believed in Him should not perish, but have everlasting life."***

God's love is a sacrificial love; He gave His only son. Not only is God's love sacrificial but also it is an unconditional love. John 3:16 also uses the word ***"whosoever"*** to indicate it is a love available to all. The last characteristic I want to give you is that God's love is a forgiving love. Colossians 3:13 reminds us:

> ***"Make allowance for each other's faults and forgive anyone who offends you. Remember, the Lord forgave you, so you must forgive others."***

I pray that we as the church would begin to be ministers of reconciliation and bridge differences with people with the love of God. After all, that is what God did for us. Our world needs to see Christians who love others sacrificially, unconditionally, and forgivingly to all we come in contact with. God has called us as believers to a ministry of reconciliation and it is time for the church to truly be the church. If we could live this way, we would help the hurting, we would bring people together, and in turn lead many to faith in Christ.

I leave you with a quote from a great preacher of times past that speaks to how we should live:

> ***"Do all the good you can, to all the people you can, in all the ways you can, as long as you can."***
> –D.L. Moody

Finding Hope in Times of Trouble

"The Lord is good, a strong refuge when trouble comes. He is close to those who trust in him."
Nahum 1:7

When trouble comes, there are plenty of people who will give you advice on what you should do and how you should do it. There are even those folks who will be quick to tell you how you managed to get yourself into trouble. All of that advice can be bothersome and all of it is a reaction to what has transpired. Rather than continually dwelling on a reaction I wanted to pose to you a plan that is proactive when it comes to trouble. This proactive approach moves us from the focus of what are we going to do and to the perspective of who are we going to trust.

I love the truth of Nahum 1:7. God is indeed good. When we step back and examine our lives we can clearly see all that the good that God has done in each of our lives. Even though we have hard times, God is still present during those times. This verse in Nahum also provides the real secret in experiencing God through difficult times. That secret is to spend our lives trusting God for the daily details of life and even more when trouble comes.

In order to trust God daily, I am convinced that our focus must change. IF you are like me, it is easy to become self-sufficient in how we live. I have found myself over the years depending on my wisdom and my judgment first before I turn to God for His wisdom. I am sad to say that when I have done this over the years that it has rarely worked for me the way I would want. Instead, I wind up frustrated and discouraged. I have come to the realization that I must change my focus off what I can do and instead focus on what God can do.

Charles Stanley illustrates this well when he states: **"When trouble comes, focus on God's ability to care for you."** What would it look like if we began to focus on God's ability to care for us when trouble comes? Nahum 1:7 answers that question so beautifully when it says that the Lord is *"close to those who trust in Him."* In essence, we will begin to sense and feel His presence and comfort.

I do not know what you may be facing today but I believe that we all need the strong refuge in God that Nahum 1:7 promises when trouble comes our way. Truly, our hope should be in the Lord on good and bad days. I have seen in my lifetime just how good God is and how much of a refuge He is when trouble appears.

I have come to the realization even though I have to be reminded at times that my focus must be on trusting God with my everyday life. It is inevitable that trouble is going to come our way in this life so let's begin to be proactive with our faith by choosing a lifestyle that ensures that we stay close to God.

For those of you today who may be during trouble, I pray that you will sense God's presence and God's provision as He enables you to weather the storm!

Overcoming Weakness

"But He said to me, 'My grace is sufficient for you, for my power is made perfect in weakness.' Therefore, I will boast all the more gladly about my weaknesses, so that Christ's power may rest on me."
2 Corinthians 12:9

Throughout history, God has chosen to use the most unlikely of people to accomplish great things. For example, God used a 13-year-old boy named David to take down a 9-foot-tall giant named Goliath. He used a man who committed murder named Moses to lead His people out of Egypt. This type of story is repeated throughout the Word of God. Have you ever wondered why He chose the relatively weak people to accomplish such great tasks?

I believe God chose the weak so that He and He alone would get the glory for what was accomplished. Imagine if God had chosen a strong and mighty warrior instead of David to take down Goliath. Many would have credited the warrior instead of God for this accomplishment.

I would dare say that many reading this today are dealing with some type of struggle in their lives. In these struggles of life, we can feel very weak and defeated. Not knowing where to find answers. There may be many of you today who are so discouraged by the struggles you face and the feelings of weakness that result.

I want you to know that God has provided another way for us and never intended for us to live defeated Christian lives. 2 Corinthians 12:9 tells us that we must learn that God's grace is sufficient for every circumstance of life. Paul reminds us in this verse that God's power shows itself so strong in our lives when we are at our weakest points.

Paul goes on to say that our attitude about our weaknesses can change from despair to joy when we allow God's power to rest on us. In Ephesians 1:19, Paul describes God's power when he says:

"I also pray that you will understand the incredible greatness of God's power for us who believe Him. This is the same mighty power that raised Christ from the dead and seated Him in the place of honor at God's right hand in the heavenly realms."

What a powerful reminder that can help us to understand the greatness of God's power that is available to those who follow Him. Paul tells us that we have access to the same power that raised Jesus from the grave to help us with any weakness or struggle we may encounter in this life.

Paul understood that his weaknesses were opportunities for God to show Himself strong. I pray that each of us will see that truth as well today. Dr. Charles Stanley encouraged me greatly years ago, in a message when he said:

> *"We can be tired, weary, and emotionally distraught, but after spending time alone with God, we find that He injects into our bodies energy, power, and strength."*

May we all move forward understanding how God would have us to overcome weakness!

No Room for Doubt

"Our heavenly Father understands our disappointment, suffering, pain, fear, and doubt. He is always there to encourage our hearts and help us understand that He's sufficient for all of our needs. When I accepted this as an absolute truth in my life, I found that my worrying stopped."
Charles Stanley

We all have periods in our lives when we doubt something or someone. During these times, life can become hard and endless worrying can become our constant companion. Webster defines doubt as **"to call into question the truth of"** something.

I remember years ago in my early twenties wondering if God really did indeed have the right someone for me to marry and spend my life with. It appeared every relationship that I entered at that time just could not materialize. I reached a point where I was filled with doubt about that part of my future.

I will never forget during that period that God gave me a verse from Psalm 94:19 that spoke to my need. That verse declares:

> *"When doubts filled my mind, your comfort gave me renewed hope and cheer."*

As I read that verse, God reminded me that all I ever really needed to do was to trust Him with every aspect of my life. It was not long after that I met who would become my wife. I have learned over the years that there is no room for doubt when we place our trust in Him.

God has promised in His Word that *"He will never leave us or forsake us."* He also promised us in Philippians 4:19 that He will:

> *"supply all your needs from his glorious riches, which have been given to us in Christ Jesus."*

I love the words of a song entitled *"More Than Enough"* written and performed by the Brooklyn Tabernacle. The words of the song point us back to who we can trust when doubt enters our lives.

> *Jehovah Jireh, my provider*
> *You are more than enough for me.*
> *Jehovah Rapha, You're my healer,*
> *by Your stripes, I've been set free.*
>
> *Jehovah Shamma, You are with me,*
> *You supply all my needs;*
>
> *You're more than enough,*
> *more than enough,*
> *more than enough for me.*

What's Your Perspective?

"Perspective is everything when you are experiencing the challenges of life."
Joni Eareckson Tada

We have all heard the expression *"perception is reality."* What it means is that for others, be they your peers, subordinates, or superiors, how they perceive something, or somebody is reality *to them*. We all face many challenges and struggles in this life that can discourage us and rob us of true joy. There are times it seems that such discouragement will overwhelm us completely. These type struggles are reality to us.

How can we gain a new perspective when we are faced with difficult times? I love the perspective of Joni Eareckson Tada above, a great Christian speaker and author, who suffered a life altering injury years ago, that left her as quadriplegic. What changed her perspective in how she sees life? The only way that Joni found the right perspective was in the person of Jesus Christ.

What about Corrie Ten Boom, a great Christian and author, who survived the Holocaust confined to a Nazi prison camp during World War II? Through all of that suffering she held onto a different perspective. She said: **"With Jesus, even in our darkest moments the best remains and the very best is yet to be..."**

What about our perspective? How are we dealing with the challenges of life? There are times that I honestly struggle with having the right perspective when trouble arises. The perspectives of Corrie Ten Boom and Joni Eareckson Tada have helped me a lot in these times.

However, my real source of strength for gaining a new perspective is found with great reminders from God's Word. There are two great principles that I want to give you that I pray will help us change our perspective. Those principles are:

1) <u>**We need to stop focusing on the size of our problem and instead focus on how big our God is!**</u>

    Jesus told us in John 16:33: *"I have told you all this so that you may have peace in me. Here on earth you will have many trials and sorrows. But take heart, because I have overcome the world."* Jesus told us that we would face difficulties in this life but He assured us that He is bigger than anything we will ever face. There is nothing that He cannot overcome.

2) <u>**We must recognize that God does have better days ahead for us!**</u>

    "For I reckon that the sufferings of this present time are not worthy to be compared with the glory which shall be revealed in us." Romans 8:18

Paul reminds us that better days are not only ahead but also more than we could ever imagine! I pray that the truths of these passages will encourage us today to help gain the perspective God desires for us to have.

Doing What Does Not Come Naturally

"Bless those who persecute you. Don't curse them; pray that God will bless them. Never pay back evil with more evil. Do things in such a way that everyone can see you are honorable."
Romans 12:14,17

We all have been hurt by different people in our lifetime. Sometimes we have even been hurt by those we have called friends and family. Some of those hurts are often the most painful. The instinct for us when we have been hurt or ridiculed is to strike back or as the verse says above to *"pay back evil with more evil."*

Our culture tells us to be mad, hold a grudge, and get even if possible. However, in the verses above, Jesus is calling us to a different standard. The ability to bless those who hurt us is counter-cultural thinking. How is that even possible? It is possible because as Christians the Bible teaches us that the Holy Spirit of God lives within each of us making it possible for us to live and react differently in these situations than most people.

If we will allow the Holy Spirit to lead and control our lives, then He will fill our hearts with too much love to hate others and hold grudges. Romans 12:17 goes on to command us to **"do things in such a way that everyone can see you are honorable."** In other words, God is instructing us to rise above what has been done to us so that others might the see the love of Jesus in our lives.

You might be thinking this is all well and good for a goal but does the Bible really understand what has happened to me. I want to remind you the verses in Romans 12 were written by a man who understood hurt and being wrongfully treated. The Apostle Paul had been beaten, stoned, and thrown in prison for living the Christian life. Paul understood what it meant to respond in a way that would honor God instead of seeking to get even.

Romans 12:18 also declares: **"If it is possible, as far as it depends on you, live at peace with everyone."** God is teaching us to respond to anger and hurt in a different manner. It is not natural to what the world expects but it is what the Lord would have us to do.

I have also learned over the years that getting even, holding a grudge, or staying angry is not a good thing for me physically or spiritually. I have found that this type of response only hurts me over the long haul. There is an anonymous quote that has helped me with my approach in handling hurt and anger.

> *"Holding onto anger is like drinking poison
> and expecting the other person to die."*

I pray God will use the truths of these verses to help those of you today that find yourselves amid some hurt you may be experiencing.

When All Else Fails

> *"We were under great pressure, far
> beyond our ability to endure."*
> *2 Corinthians 1:8*

Last August, we experienced a rare total solar eclipse of the sun. On that day, the moon stood between the sun and earth blocking out most of the sunlight from the earth. The moon worked that day to cause darkness at an unusual time of the day. Similarly, there are many times in life when we encounter problems and difficulties that cause us to experience dark times.

The truth is that life can be so hard at times. There are times during the trials of life that it appears there is little that we can depend upon. Paul describes in the verse above how we feel many times when he says, **"we were under great pressure, far beyond our ability to endure."** Some of you who are reading this article may be feeling that pressure right now.

As a Christian, the Bible provides us with hope when all else fails. I want to remind each of us today of the hope that God gives us for this life.

1) <u>**God pours His love on us each day!**</u>

> *"But each day the* LORD *pours his unfailing love upon me and through each night I sing His songs, praying to God who gives me life."*

This verse reminds us that God ***"pours His unfailing love on us each day."*** An unfailing love is one that will be there when all else fails. We need to be reminded of this truth regularly. When we remember this, God will put a song in our heart and prayer will once again become the first place we run to in time of trouble.

2) <u>**God sends new mercies every day!**</u>
> *"Great is His faithfulness; His mercies begin afresh each morning."* **Lamentations 3:23**

I am grateful that we can start each day with a new set of mercies for that day. What a blessing to know that when all else fails that God offers us new hope for each day that we face.

3) <u>**God is with you no matter what!**</u>
> *"When you go through deep waters I will be with you."* **Isaiah 43:2**

This verse provides us with the promise that no matter who else may desert us we should always remember that God is with us in every circumstance. He stands there with us providing love, hope, and encouragement for all the challenges that this life brings.

I ran across something that Charles Stanley once said about trials that I pray will serve as reminder to all of us in how we approach them.

> *"Every test, every trial, every heartache that's been significant, I can turn it over and see how God has turned it into good no matter what."*

My prayer is that this will give us all hope when all else fails!

Tapping into The Right Source of Strength

"In your strength, I can crush an army;
with my God I can scale any wall."
2 Samuel 22:30

I have often been asked by parents what are some of the most important things that you can teach your children in this life. First, I always tried to teach my children to love God with all their heart, soul, and mind as Scripture says. I also wanted to teach them that following God is a daily process that requires spending time in His Word and in prayer. Indeed, I wanted to teach them to run hard after God.

Beyond that, I knew that my wife and I had the responsibility to teach our children to one day be independent of us and dependent on God. For them to learn to stand on their own feet, I knew it would be necessary to teach them where to find the right source of strength for living in this world.

We wanted to teach them first that God is with them no matter what they face. Matthew 28:20 tells us:

"And be sure of this: I am with you always,
even to the end of the age."

Next, we felt it important that our children learn that tapping into God's strength is imperative for living this life. The biggest mistake that most Christians, including myself, make in this life is trying to do everything in our own strength. An even bigger mistake we make as parents is continuing to do everything for our children and solving all their problems as they get older.

Trying to solve all of life's issues ourselves in our strength clearly does not work and only works to discourage us in the long run. We must teach and live the truth of Philippians 4:13 to our children.

> *"For I can do everything through Christ,
> who gives me strength."*

Finally, as we learn to tap into God's strength and teach that principle to our children we will soon see just how powerful our God really is. 2 Samuel 22:30 above tells us that with God anything is possible. I love how it declares that *"with my God, I can scale any wall."*

What greater truth could we teach our kids than this? I believe that it is the heart of every parent to see our kids accomplish great things and find true fulfillment for their lives. I do not know about you, but I have always wanted my kids to be able to scale any wall or obstacle this life puts in their way.

May God grant us as parents the wisdom to teach our kids to tap into God's strength for this life. Not only that, but also give us the strength to let them use God's strength and not ours as they get older so that they will learn to be independent of us and dependent on our great God!

Don't Have to Be Afraid

> *"For God has not given us a spirit of fear and
> timidity, but of power, love, and self-discipline."*
> 2 Timothy 1:7

When my youngest daughter was 3 years old, she went through a period where she was terribly afraid at night. Because of this fear, she would come into our bedroom at night and sleep beside our bed. Once there, she would want to hold my hand until she felt asleep. She needed the security of someone to hold onto to when she was afraid.

As adults, we too have many times when fear grips us and we ache for a feeling of security and peace. God's Word reminds us that He never intended for His children to live in fear. 1 Timothy 1:7 tells us that He has not ***"given us a spirit of fear and timidity."*** Paul was speaking to Timothy when he gave this verse. In V5-6 of that same chapter, he is reminding Timothy that because of of his genuine, growing faith he did not have to be afraid or timid.

In fear's place, this verse tells us that we have instead ***"power, love, and self-discipline."*** What does Paul mean by this? What kind of power is he referring to? I believe that this power is the one that Paul spoke of in Ephesians 1:19-20 when he said:

> ***"I also pray that you will understand the incredible greatness of God's power for us who believe him. This is the same mighty power that raised Christ from the dead and seated him in the place of honor at God's right hand in the heavenly realms."***

My prayer is that we might truly understand as this verse the greatness of God's power in our lives. It is the power that raised Jesus from the dead. Instead of fear, God has given us His incredible power in which to live our lives.

What kind of love is He referring to? I believe he is talking about a John 3:16 love that declares: ***"For God so loved the world that He gave..."*** kind of love. He has given us a love that is sacrificial and unconditional. That is a love that ***"casts out fear."***

Finally, one of the fruits of the Spirit God has given us is self-control. If we will put our hope in Him and not this world, then we gain self-control over whatever comes against us. I love how 1 Peter 1:13 describes this truth:

"So prepare your minds for action and exercise self-control. Put all your hope in the gracious salvation that will come to you when Jesus Christ is revealed to the world."

We do not have to be afraid! God has promised us so much more!

Chapter 7
Success

A Commitment to Success

"Commit your actions to the Lord, and
your plans will succeed."
Proverbs 16:3

There has been many a book written on how to achieve success in this life. Many of the books give you ways to improve who you are and what you are doing all with the idea of making a person rich and famous. I know that material wealth and worldly success are not enough to satisfy a person's deepest needs and desires. At the heart of every person is the need for peace in our hearts and a knowledge that we are making a difference.

God has a purpose and a plan for our lives that is much bigger than achieving the world's definition of success. God desires that we commit our lives and our actions to Him daily. God is calling us as Christians to live for a purpose that is so much bigger than who we are. I believe with all my heart that giving our kids a transcendent purpose or living for something bigger (God) is the greatest thing we can teach them.

We spend so much time in our lives making plans and planning for the future. We do the same with our children as we are focused on helping them to achieve success in life. There is nothing inherently wrong with that idea. However, I believe that Proverbs 16:3 gives us a better way to approach life and planning. Instead of spending so much time on planning, this verse I think is challenging us to spend more time on finding God's purpose for our lives and then committing all of our actions to His glory.

I ran across a quote that illustrates this idea so well. Myles Munroe said: ***"God's purpose is more important than our plans."*** Finding God's purpose for our lives will meet the greatest needs of our life in finding the peace and hope that people desperately seek. More than that, it will bring a sense of satisfaction that money and worldly success will never provide.

In fact, Proverbs 16:3 tells us that if we commit our actions to the Lord then our plans will succeed. What is the success here that is being referred to? I believe that it is a Godly success that is characterized by fruits of the Spirit such as love, joy, peace, contentment and so much more that only God can give.

When we commit our lives and actions to God, everything about our lives will change. I meet so many people who are tired and discouraged from the rat race of life and in trying to find success. Proverbs 16:3 is showing us a different way to live. Who does not want to find success?

The greatest thing about committing our actions to the Lord is that it is the only way to gain a success that is lasting. God sent His Son Jesus so that may experience life to the fullest not only in this lifetime but also in the eternity that is to come!

I pray that Proverbs 16:3 will encourage you today and inspire you to make a commitment to success God's way.

How to Succeed in All You Do

"Study this Book of Instruction continually. Meditate on it day and night so you will be sure to obey everything written in it. Only then will you prosper and succeed in all you do."
Joshua 1:8

Most people I know want to succeed in life. We work hard at succeeding and then we also sacrifice to give our children all the opportunities we can for them one day to succeed. This is such an overriding issue that we are constantly looking for help on how to succeed.

Joshua 1:8 provides the answer on how to succeed. That verse tells us that we are to take seriously the spiritual discipline of Bible study and application. Joshua instructs us to study God's Word continually, meditate on it constantly, and obey completely what it tells us to do. Only then, Joshua says will we prosper and succeed in all we do.

What does this really look like in our daily lives? We must be committed to doing three things:

Hearing God's Word

> *"So faith comes from hearing, and hearing by the word of Christ."*
> ***Romans 10:17***

Most Christians should be able to discipline themselves to attend church regularly and to listen to messages via radio or media. Are you committed to being in church so that you can hear God's word regularly from God's man?

Reading God's Word

> *"But He answered and said, "It is written, MAN SHALL NOT LIVE ON BREAD ALONE, BUT ON EVERY WORD THAT PROCEEDS OUT OF THE MOUTH OF GOD."*
> ***Matt 4:4***

Studies show that less than 15% of Christians read their Bible daily. Worse yet, a large majority of Christians only open their Bibles at church or very minimally during the week.

Studying and Obeying God's Word

"For Ezra had set his heart to study the law of the LORD*, and to practice it, and to teach His statutes and ordinances in Israel."*
Ezra 7:10

Ezra purposed in his heart to study God's Word, to obey it, and to teach it. He made up his mind and he disciplined himself to make Bible study and application the priority of his life. Ezra did not waffle on the issue of being in the Word of God. He knew the value of doing it and committed his life to it. What about us? Is it not time that we set our hearts towards God's Word and not allowing it to be anything other than our top priority?

From Joshua 1:8, we know that establishing this discipline will change our lives. We will see success in what we do. It will not be success as the world defines it but it will be success as God defines it. That is the only kind of success that guarantees to bring us peace, joy, contentment, love, and so much more. That kind of success will help us to lead our kids to a faith that will bless them in this life and guarantee their eternal destiny. Who does not want that kind of success?

What's keeping you from setting your heart to study, obey, and teach God's Word? I pray we will all see the value of prioritizing the spiritual discipline of Bible study and application in our lives!

Chapter 8
A Passion for the Lord

Stirred Up

"For this reason, I remind you to kindle afresh the gift of God, which is in you through the laying on of hands."
- 2 Timothy 1:6

One of my least favorite chores in the world is to paint. I do not like to paint. However, I have chosen to do this chore a lot over the years because I do not want to pay someone else to do it. I am a very results-oriented person so once it is time to paint then my mindset is to get the job done.

Many times, I have made the mistake of not properly stirring the paint up before starting. When this happens, the paint does not cover properly, and I waste a lot of effort.

I believe that the same thing can happen to us spiritually. It can be easy for us to fall into a rut spiritually and just seemingly going through the motions. All the while we are wasting a lot of effort. God's Word addresses this when Paul tells us in 2 Timothy 1:6 to **"kindle afresh"** the gift of God. **"Kindle afresh"** means to stir up.

When we are not stirred up spiritually, we do not experience the fullness in our lives that God promised. Essentially, we are just barely covering the gaps of our lives. I believe that God intended so much more for us. That is why the Apostle Paul is reminding us to stir ourselves up spiritually. What does it look like to stir ourselves up spiritually?

It is not to manufacture a feeling within ourselves but instead that we would experience the fullness of our gifting's in Christ. In this verse,

Paul is talking to Timothy and it is not that Timothy is not living correctly. Paul is reminding Timothy to keep his spiritual fire burning.

We keep our spiritual fire burning by daily spending time in God's Word and in prayer. To keep our fire burning, we must prioritize our relationship with God over all others. As we do this, we will begin to develop a passion for the things of God and for chasing after things that please Him. We will begin to really fulfill our calling and fully utilize our gifts.

You see the church today is not lacking gifted preachers, teachers, or impressive technology. Rather, it lacks people of God who are stirred up and eager to fulfill His purpose. I ran across a statement years ago that speaks to this issue. That statement was: ***"If the devil cannot keep you from getting saved, he will work to keep you average."*** I am not sure who said it, but it is so true.

Are you stirred up for the Lord? Are you experiencing a fresh move of the Spirit in your life? I pray this verse will speak to your heart!

Time to Let the World Know

"On this day the L<small>ORD</small> *will deliver you into my hands, and I'll strike you down and cut off your head. This very day I will give the carcasses of the Philistine army to the birds and the wild animals, and the whole world will know that there is a God in Israel."*
- 1 Samuel 17:46

At the age of 13, David faced the biggest giant of his life when he faced Goliath. Goliath was a striking 9 feet tall and he had been daily taunting the soldiers of the Israelite army. None of those soldiers were wanting to face Goliath. In fact, they ran away and hid rather than face this giant. Young David came along and knew that this giant should not be allowed to mock not only the army of God but God Himself.

David knew in his heart that God would deliver this giant into his hands. I love his statement to Goliath from verse 46 above in which he tells the giant that *"on this day"* he will kill Goliath. What I love even more is that he wants the giant to know that as a result of this that the whole world will know that there is a God in Heaven. David's trust in God would bring honor, glory, and fame to God and God alone.

What if we would live in such a way? We all face giants in life that can overwhelm us and cause us like the Israelite army to run away. I am convinced that we need to take David's approach to facing the giants of life. What exactly did David do?

1) **First, David trusted God to deliver him from this giant.**
   In 1 Samuel 17:37, David told King Saul that God will *"deliver me out of the hand of this Philistine."* We all need to be reminded that God is working on our behalf to provide strength, hope, and even deliverance form the giants we face.

2) **Next, David armed himself to face this giant.**
   1 Samuel 17:40 tells us that David chose 5 smooth stones not the King's armor to face the giant. David took on the armor that God had provided him in the past to overcome giants. We all need to take on the armor God daily with his Word and His Spirit to face our giants.

3) **David faced the giant head on with great confidence.**
   David was determined that there would be no running away, no procrastinating, and no putting it off on someone else. He faced that giant head on with confidence in the Lord and not himself. I pray today that when faced with giants that we too could face our giants with confidence in God. Please remember

as 1 John 4:4 tells us *"**greater is He that is in you than he who is in the world.**"*

4) **Finally, David wanted to make sure that everyone knew that God gets the credit.**
   I pray that we too would live in a way that gives honor and glory to God through the struggles and battles of life.

It is time to let the world know that we serve an awesome God who will help us with any giant we may face in this lifetime. As the old preacher used to say, ***"the things that are over our heads are already under His feet."*** May the world see this truth lived out in our everyday walk.

Getting Strong without Steroids

"Search for the Lord and for his strength; continually seek him."
1 Chronicles 16:11

In recent years, we have all seen the highly publicized stories of superstar athletes who have been caught using steroids and thus have had to forfeit awards and endured public scorn. Steroids have been used by people over the years to grow strong at a very quick rate and to gain advantage over others. The truth is that there is no real shortcut to getting strong physically. To do so, requires discipline, hard work, commitment, and long hours.

The same principle holds true for us spiritually. There are no shortcuts to growing spiritually. As 1 Chronicles 16:11 says above, we are to continually or throughout our lives seek the Lord and His strength. If we are to be strong in the Lord, this is a process that will never end if we live on this earth. As we seek Him, I am convinced that God will change our hearts, our perspective, and our view of where our real strength comes from. Let me share with you some of the benefits of finding our strength in the Lord.

First, I believe that the real source of strength for our lives comes from developing an intimate relationship with God. This relationship will provide us with a real joy that many times is missing from our daily lives. Nehemiah 8:10 tells us that *"**the joy of the Lord is your strength!**"* I am sure that each of us would love to have this type of abiding joy that permeates our lives regardless for the circumstances that come our way.

Next, God promises in Isaiah 40:29 that He will give *"**power to the weak and strength to the powerless.**"* In other words, we face so many situations that seem so far beyond our own power and in those times, God promises to give us the strength to face whatever challenge may be upon us.

Finally, I saved the best part of finding our strength in the Lord until the last. In 2 Samuel 22:30 the Bible tells us that *"**In your strength I can crush an army; with my God I can scale any wall.**"* With God, there is nothing that is impossible. We do not have to rely any longer on what we alone can do. The circumstances of life do not have to win or control us.

I love the phrase that *"**with my God I can scale any wall.**"* This reminds me that there is no dream or goal that is too big for our God. There is no hope or aspiration that is beyond what our God can do if it His will for our lives. This is indeed a strength that is beyond what any human effort can ever produce.

What walls are you facing today? What obstacles are in your way? Are you tired of trying to overcome these things in your own strength? I know what that feels like as I have been there many times. I pray that each of us will seek the Lord and His strength for our lives so that we can start to scale the walls we are facing in God's strength alone.

May we all begin to experience as Nehemiah did that *"the joy of the Lord is our strength.*

Instruction You Never Forget

"These were his instructions to them: "You must always act in the fear of the Lord, with faithfulness and an undivided heart."
2 Chronicles 19:9

I am so grateful to God for giving me two of the Godliest and most loving parents a child could ever ask for. They gave me a lot of instruction and much of it I have never forgotten. I will always remember a very powerful lesson that my mother taught me when I was about 5 years old.

This lesson occurred on vacation when my mother had taken me down to the ocean for a swim. We had to cross a very busy street on foot. My mother instructed me to hold her hand and to not move until she told me to. On that day, I was barefoot having just come from the beach. My feet began to hurt fiercely from the heat to the point that I could not stand waiting any longer. Immediately, I let go of my mother's hand and darted across the street. I narrowly avoided being hit by a car. Looking back, I know that my protection that day was the providence of God.

I know that I had scared my mother to death. However, my mother's emotions quickly swung from relief that I was not hurt to anger at me for disobeying. I got a spanking that I will never forget but I also got instruction that has lasted me a lifetime. My mother shared with me then and since then how much she loves me and how important it is that I obey. That incident taught me how important it is to hold on to what is important and always act a certain way. It taught the importance of obedience and faithfulness. I have never forgotten the lessons of that day.

In 2 Chronicles 19, King Jehosophat went about giving instruction to his people that he knew would serve them well. The King gave three instructions in verse nine of that chapter to his people. These three instructions are:

1) **Always act in the fear of the Lord**
2) **Be faithful**
3) **Have an undivided heart**

You see, once we learn to fear the Lord then we must daily act in that manner. It is not enough to say that I fear the Lord and be done with the statement. We must daily be in His Word and spend time with Him so that we will always act in the fear of the Lord. If we take in God's Word daily and allow it to permeate our lives, it will change the way we act. God can change us to the point that we will ***"always act in the fear of the Lord."***

Next, we are instructed to be faithful. As I mentioned earlier, a healthy fear of my mother helped me in the future to learn to be faithful to what she asked me to do. It was fear that was birthed out of love for her. The same holds true of our relationship with God. When we learn to fear Him, we will love Him so much that we will desire to be faithful.

Finally, the fear of the Lord and a love for the Lord will lead us to where we can have an undivided heart. The instruction from King Jehosophat is clear. We are to have an undivided heart so that our passion, our loyalty, our love, and our devotion are to God and God alone. King Jehosophat's instructions are so powerful. I pray that these will be instructions that we will never forget.

Chapter 9
What the World Needs Now!

How to Enjoy Life

"If you want to enjoy life and see many happy days, keep your tongue from speaking evil and your lips from telling lies. Turn away from evil and do good. Search for peace, and work to maintain it."
1 Peter 3:10-11

Everyone remembers the key phrase from the Declaration of independence which says:

"We hold these truths to be self-evident, that all men are created equal, that they are endowed by their Creator with certain unalienable Rights, that among these are Life, Liberty and the pursuit of Happiness."

We are blessed to be Americans and live in this great country. I especially love the statement the *"pursuit of happiness."* We are free to pursue happiness. In fact, I believe most if not all people long for happiness. We long to enjoy life.

! Peter 3:10-11 gives us incredible insight into what enjoying life may look like. That passage tells if we want to enjoy and life and many happy days then we must do a few things. First, we must learn to control our tongue. How do we do that?

I believe that we must stay close to God through the reading of His Word and spending time with Him in prayer. I am convinced that if we make Him the focus of our lives we will be different. His Word will change our focus, or speech, and our conduct. How do I know His Word will change our speech? Look at Hebrews 4:12 and Isaiah 55:11 below.

> *"For the word of God is alive and powerful. It is sharper than the sharpest two-edged sword, cutting between soul and spirit, between joint and marrow. It exposes our innermost thoughts and desires."*

> *"It is the same with my word. I send it out, and it always produces fruit. It will accomplish all I want it to, and it will prosper everywhere I send it."*

Spending time in His Word will keep us from speaking evil and will instead enable us to uplift others with our speech. 1 Peter 3:10-11 also reminds us that we should seek peace with others and **"work to maintain it."** Romans 12:18 also instructs us to:

> *"Do all that you can to live in peace with everyone."*

From this passage, we are taught that to enjoy lie and see many happy days then we are to control our tongue and seek peace with others. As I thought about this truth, I see the wisdom in what God could truly do for my life by submitting to this. Most of the problems I encounter are when I do not control my tongue and look to live in peace. More importantly, this reminds me finding real joy and happiness begins with me committing my life to God and following His Word. God will honor that kind of lifestyle. 1 Peter 3:12 confirms this when it declares:

> *"The eyes of the Lord watch over those who do right, and his ears are open to their prayers. But the Lord turns his face against those who do evil."*

What the World Needs Now

"Don't pretend to love others. Really love them. Hate what is wrong. Hold tightly to what is good." Romans 12:9

There is popular song from years ago that declared that *"what the world needs now is love, sweet love. It's the only thing that there's just too little of. What the world needs now is love, sweet love. No not just for some but for everyone."* As popular as that song was at the time, the need for love is even greater in the world in which we live today.

Indeed, we live in a culture in which we see too much hate and evil. Unfortunately, many times this hate and evil is perpetuated by people who claim to be Christians or in the name of Christianity. I am convinced that it is time for those of us who know Christ as our personal Lord and Savior to show this world what the love of God really looks like.

Let's be clear about what the love of God does not look like. The love of God has no part in racism and hatred. Extremist groups and white supremacist groups are not of God. The Bible is clear on these issues. The verses below tell us that hatred of others is clearly not of God nor indicative of His love.

"If a man say, I love God, and hateth his brother, he is a liar: for he that loveth not his brother whom he hath seen, how can he love God whom he hath not seen?"
1 John 4:20

"He that loves not knows not God; for God is love."
1 John 4:8

Acts 10:34 also tells us that God does not regard any one person or group above another: *"I see very clearly that God shows no favoritism. In every nation, He accepts those who fear Him and do what is right."*

The love of God should be evident in the lives of Christ followers. 1 John 4:11 tells us that: *"If God so loved us, we ought also to love one another."* God sent His precious Son to die on a cruel Roman cross so that we might have life abundant and eternal. How much then should we allow the love of God to permeate our lives in how we treat others?

In conclusion, it is time as Romans 12:9 says for the world to see that followers of Christ *"hate what is wrong and hold tightly to what is good."* It is also time according to that verse for Christians to allow the Holy Spirit of God to produce the spirit of love in us so that we can stop pretending and really begin to love others. This is the kind of love that the world needs now.

Dealing with Conflict

We all have those times in our lives when we do not get along with someone else. Those times come as early as preschool and last up until death. Some conflicts can get quite intense and others are simply disagreements that we must learn to deal with.

The Bible provides great principles for helping us deal with conflict. These principles are also needed in teaching our children how to deal with conflict.

I am amazed at times when folks tell me about *"irreconcilable differences."* I go onto to tell them that there is no such thing because the greatest irreconcilable difference that ever existed was between God and man but God sent His Son Jesus to bridge that gap. Therefore, there are no irreconcilable differences only stubborn, unforgiving people.

So how can we deal with conflict Biblically? First, we need to learn the Matthew 18 principle for resolving conflict. Matthew 18:15-16 advises us:

"If another believer sins against you, go privately and point out the offense. If the other person listens and confesses it, you have won that person back. But if you are unsuccessful, take one or two others with you and go back again, so that everything you say may be confirmed by two or three witnesses."

These verses teach us that our first action in a conflict is to approach the other person involved to resolve the conflict. We should go to them in love first and not go to others. We should not post on social media how we have been offended but go directly to the source in love.

The verses also give us direction if that does not work. It directs us then to ask a Godly person or two to join us in going back to the other party to work towards resolution. The caution I would share here is to not make a small dispute into something bigger than it needs to be.

Another principle that is important to remember is to be kind and forgiving remembering that God forgives you. Ephesians 4:32 instructs us to: **"Instead, be kind to each other, tenderhearted, forgiving one another, just as God through Christ has forgiven you."**

We should be quick to apologize for any role we may have in the dispute. Not only should we apologize but we should also be quick to forgive and forget and not to hold grudges. Mark 11:25 is a key principle to teach: **"But when you are praying, first forgive anyone you are holding a grudge against, so that your Father in heaven will forgive your sins, too."**

Finally, we also should remember that there will be conflicts that some folks will just not want to resolve. We should forgive them anyways and still be kind. This is indeed how the Lord would have us deal with conflict.

The Right Mindset

We are given the command in Scripture to love the Lord your God with *"all our mind."* We also need to model and teach this same command to our children. Unfortunately, the world we live in today operates with a very dualistic mindset. What do I mean by dualism? Webster defines dualism as: *"the quality or state of having two different or opposite parts or elements."*

What does this look like today in our world? People live and behave one way in church and around Christians and then go off during the week with a different mindset that characterizes them in their workplace and other settings. For the most part, dualism describes a lifestyle that is compartmentalized depending on where we are and what we are doing.

God never intended for us to live this way. He never intended for us to be double minded. James 1:8 tells us that *"a double-minded man is unstable in all his ways."*

What does this look like in the real world? Being double minded explains how I can see people on social media one day post a Bible verse and proclaim how God is their life and a day later curse and swear on that same social media site. James 3:9-12 tells us that this lifestyle should not happen in the life of a believer.

"Out of the same mouth proceed blessing and cursing. My brethren, these things ought not to be so. Does a spring send forth fresh water and bitter from the same opening? Can a fig tree, my brethren, bear olives, or a grapevine bear figs? Thus, no spring yields both salt water and fresh."

Our goal must be to provide an environment for our children that destroys the idea of a dual lifestyle. How are we going to integrate truth into every area of our child's daily experience so that we can not only prevent a dualistic mindset but more importantly develop a Biblical worldview in our kids?

1) **Teach Your Kids The things of God Daily**
   "Repeat them again and again to your children. Talk about them when you are at home and when you are on the road, when you are going to bed and when you are getting up."
   Deuteronomy 6:7

   Make sure that you continually teach a Biblical worldview so that no other alternative way of thinking emerges. If our kids' minds are trained in Scripture they can quickly disregard false ideas and methods.

2) **Model the Right Mindset for Our Kids**
   In Philippians 3:17, Paul declared: ***"Dear brothers and sisters, pattern your lives after mine, and learn from those who follow our example.*** As parents, we must become students of the Word who daily rely on it for our direction in all of life's decisions. Our children need to see us living and modeling a Biblical lifestyle. I pray that we would be able to have our kids follow our example.

I pray that these principles will be helpful to you as you work to provide your children with the right mindset!

Different Kind of Courage

We live in some very difficult times in which we have seen much of our traditional family values come under attack. I have been dismayed as the Supreme Court has ruled in favor of same sex marriage this summer and as I watch traditional families crumbling all around us. With all this happening how should we react? What should we do?

I want to bring your attention to Nehemiah and how he approached troubling times in his world. He showed great courage in leading his people in difficult times. When Nehemiah returned to Jerusalem, he found the city in great trouble and disgrace. Nehemiah 1:3-4 tells us of Nehemiah's reaction.

> *"They said to me, "Things are not going well for those who returned to the province of Judah. They are in great trouble and disgrace. The wall of Jerusalem has been torn down, and the gates have been destroyed by fire. When I heard this, I sat down and wept. In fact, for days I mourned, fasted, and prayed to the God of heaven."*

With a broken heart, Nehemiah went directly to God and sought God's wisdom for dealing with the situation around him. Nehemiah was broken before the Lord on behalf of the people and the situation. After seeking the Lord, he went about with a plan to rebuild. I am convinced that this kind of leadership is needed today to engage the culture in which we live. We must allow God to break us and bring us to the point that we will follow Him completely and allow Him to direct our paths.

I read recently something by Warren Wiersbe that echoes this thought. Wiersbe stated: ***"I hear people saying, we need angry leaders today! The time has come to practice militant Christianity! Perhaps, but the "wrath of man does not produce the righteousness of God". What we need to day is not anger but anguish. The difference between anger and anguish is a broken heart."***

May God grant us the courage today to allow ourselves to be broken over what is going on in our world but also that He might fill us with His love and His heart towards people? May we seek God and get His wisdom for engaging our culture. I really believe it is time for committed Christians to love people as Christ would have us to regardless of what they believe.

Unfortunately, Christians are better known for what we are against than what we are for. Throughout the earthly ministry of Jesus, He would be found ministering and loving those who were the most broken. I pray that we as followers of Christ would allow God to mold our hearts so that we sound a whole lot less like cable news and a whole lot more like Jesus.

Indeed, we live in a broken and messy world that needs Jesus. I pray that God will give us the courage to live the Christian life undivided and with a passion to tell others with great love of the marvelous grace of our Lord. If we want to change the course of our culture, the process must begin with God doing a work in our hearts.

I believe that if we as Christians would have the courage to live committed Christian lives with a loving Christ-like heart then I am convinced we will have the opportunity to see revival in our country and reverse the trends we see in culture.

Will you join me in praying for revival and most importantly that the revival would begin with each of us!

Chapter 10
Choosing Wisely

Our Lives Are Determined by the Choices We Make

"And a small rudder makes a huge ship turn wherever the pilot chooses to go, even though the winds are strong."
James 3:4

I find it so fascinating that one of the smaller parts of the ship, the rudder, has such a huge impact on the direction of a ship. This verse reminds us that the rudder can steer the ship in any direction the pilot chooses regardless of how strong the wind is blowing. Our hearts are like the rudder that is described in the book of James.

The focus and affections of our heart determine our direction. A heart that is focused and fixed on the things of this world will follow the cultural winds that are blowing today. The winds of this culture are on a path that takes us further away from God and further away from truth. These winds have led our society to issues such as the highest divorce rate in history, the highest suicide rate in history, and more people who say that they are discontented than ever before.

A heart that is fixed and anchored in the hope of Jesus Christ can help us steer through the difficult winds that are blowing in our culture. This type of heart can lead us to find significance in the only one who can really provide significance to our lives.

I am convinced that ultimately the direction of our lives will be determined by the choices we make daily. Serving and living for God is a choice we must make daily. Submitting our wills and our desires to Him is a choice we must make daily. The little choices we make each day either lead us closer in our walk with God or take us further away.

Why is this important? For one, John 10:10 Jesus tells us that *"I have come that you might have life and have it more abundantly."* Anchoring our heart to Jesus Christ is believing that He and He alone can provide that abundant life that He promised. I have personally found this to be true. Nothing this world can offer has ever given me the abundant life that Jesus spoke of in John. Only living for Him has ever given me peace, joy, strength, contentment, hope, and so much more.

Next, these choices not only have such a huge impact on the direction of our lives but also the direction of kids' lives. Our children are watching and will follow much of what we model. I want my children to experience the abundant life Jesus promised. I want them to commit their hearts (rudders) to Jesus so that they too can steer through the storms of this life.

Because of these two reasons, I want my heart (rudder) committed to following Jesus and living for Him. What about you? I had someone tell me recently that they have wasted so much of life through bad choices. Let me encourage any of you today who feel that way with a quote from Max Lucado.

"The meaning of life. The wasted years of life. The poor choices of life. God answers the mess of life with one word: 'grace'."

Wow! The marvelous grace of our Lord and Savior Jesus Christ is there for all of us to have a new start and a new direction no matter the choices we have made in the past. I pray that we will all fix our hearts on Jesus and allow Him to steer us through the devastating winds of this culture.

Completely His

"For the eyes of the Lord move to and fro and throughout the earth that He may strongly support those whose heart is completely His."
2 Chronicles 16:9

We are living in some very difficult days in which we have seen traditional family values and Christianity come under attack. In addition, we have seen the rise of many unthinkable and evil acts against our fellow man. Our world seems at times in shambles. What should be the role of Christians to reverse this trend?

First, I am convinced that we as believers and followers of Christ must individually recommit our hearts completely to Christ. We need to get back in His Word like never before. As well, we must begin to pray as never before. We need God's direction on how to make a difference in this culture. From time in the Word and time on our knees, I believe that God will give us a vision to impact our world.

Author Chip Ingram has a great definition of vision that speaks to this issue. Ingram states that: ***"Vision is a God-given burden to see what a person, a place, or a situation could become if the grace of God and the power of God were unleashed on them."***

Can you imagine if we would give our hearts completely to God and then allow Him to work through us to love people and continually share the good news of the Gospel with all around us? If we could get a God-given burden like this, 2 Chronicles 16:9 tells us that this is something that God is not only looking for, but it is also a burden that He will support.

You see the truth is that when our hearts are completely His, then we will begin to chase after the pursuits of life that He would have us chase after. Our world desperately needs to see authentic Christianity and the love of Christ. My prayer is that this will be a year in which we as a staff at Metrolina will model this for our students and families as never before.

Also, that we would ask God for a God-given burden for our culture and that from that burden we will develop a plan that will allow God to unleash His grace and power. I love studying Nehemiah as a leader. He encountered a culture much like today and I especially love his challenge to his people in Nehemiah 2:17-18.

> *"But now I said to them, "You know very well what trouble we are in. Jerusalem lies in ruins, and its gates have been destroyed by fire. Let us rebuild the wall of Jerusalem and end this disgrace!" Then I told them about how the gracious hand of God had been on me, and about my conversation with the king." They replied at once, "Yes, let's rebuild the wall!" So they began the good work."*

These verses reveal Nehemiah's God-given burden to rebuild the city and culture. May God give us that same type of burden for our world. Let's rebuild together so that we might bring glory to God and hope to our fellow man!

It begins with making our hearts *"Completely His"*.

How We Manage Our Time

"If you don't have time to do it right, when will you have time to do it over?"
John Wooden

One of the greatest spiritual disciplines that we all must learn is that of stewardship. We hear that word a lot and most times we assume it means how we manage our money. Stewardship is more than just money. Webster defines stewardship as *"the careful and responsible management of something entrusted to one's care."*

Time is one of those areas that God has entrusted us with to be good stewards over. Each day that we live on this earth God has provided us 86,400 seconds in which for us to be good stewards with. The Bible has a lot to say about time and how we should use it and view it. Below are a few of the things the Bible tells us about time:

1) <u>*Time is Short*</u>
   "How do you know what your life will be like tomorrow? Your life is like the morning fog— it's here a little while, then it's gone.
   "James 4:14

2) <u>*Time is Uncertain*</u>
   Don't brag about tomorrow since you don't know what the day will bring."
   Proverbs 27:1

3) <u>*Time Cannot Be Regained*</u>
   "We must quickly carry out the tasks assigned us by the one who sent us. The night is coming, and then no one can work.
   "John 9:4

4) <u>*Time is Passing*</u>
   "And this world is fading away, along with everything that people crave. But anyone who does what pleases God will live forever."
   1 John 2:17

5) *Time Defeats Evil*
"*So be careful how you live. Don't live like fools, but like those who are wise. Make the most of every opportunity in these evil days.*"
Ephesians 5:15-16

6) *Time is Highly Valued by God*
"*Yes, each of us will give a personal account to God.*"
Romans 14:12

As I look back, I am amazed at just how fast life has gone for me. It seems like only yesterday that my children were babies and now they are grown. James 4:14 is right when it says that life is like a vapor or a fog that appears for a short time and then disappears.

My heart's desire is that I would learn to be a good steward with my time. I want to embrace each day that God gives me with a passion to serve Him and know Him. I also want to be a good steward of the time that God has given me to be with my family so that they might know how much I love and cherish them. I also want to be a good steward of the time that God gives me to shepherd the students of Metrolina Christian Academy.

How are we managing the time that God has given each of us? Are we using the time we have to bring God glory? Are we prioritizing our time with God so that we might grow closer to Him? What kind of stewards are we with our time when it comes to our families? These are all questions we need to stop and ask ourselves on a regular basis.

I pray we will all begin to practice good stewardship of the time God has given each of us.

Time to Laugh

"So I recommend having fun, because there is nothing better for people in this world than to eat, drink, and enjoy life. That way they will experience some happiness along with all the hard work God gives them under the sun."
Ecclesiastes 8:15

When is the last time that you had a great laugh? My fondest memories of growing up were the times that my parents spent with me and my siblings having a good time. I will never forget the great fellowship times we would have around the dinner table. Those memories are priceless to me today.

This world and the problems that come with it can easily suck the laughter out of our lives. My parents taught me something very important growing up that I am trying to pass onto my children. They taught me to learn to laugh at myself and the adventures and troubles I find myself in.

Solomon tells us in the verse above that there is nothing better for people in this world than to enjoy life. There is also nothing better than for our children to see us not so serious at times.

My children love for me to tell them stories of the good ole days and especially a story that will create laughter. Most of those stories involve me doing something let's say not so bright. One of their favorites is when I would tell the story of what happened to me the day I went and got the marriage license so that their mom and I could get married. In the story, I tell them how I was so captivated looking at the license and the seriousness of getting married that I forgot to watch where I was going and walked into a concrete overhang and nearly knocked myself out. I go onto tell them how my dad would kid me when I got home that running into that overhang might be a sign from God about getting married.

You might ask what the point here is. The point is that I have always wanted my children to know what it means to not be so serious all the time. Our children need a home where it is okay to have a good time and laugh. There are plenty of times to be serious but we must intentionally set our hearts for joy.

Through the years, Christians have much of Psalm 66:1 which instructs us to: **"Make a joyful noise unto God, all ye lands."** We all assume that should always mean singing praise back to the Lord. Let me propose to you that it also could mean laughter. When you think about it, is there a more joyful noise than laughter? I am reminded how joyful a noise it is every time I hear my children laugh uncontrollably.

I do not want my children to look back one day and think of me as only this serious guy who never had any fun with them. I want them instead to cherish the times we had together when we laughed so hard that we almost cried. I want our family to truly make a joyful noise together. I pray also that my kids will take this idea of choosing joy and one day pass that legacy onto their families.

The idea here is that we need to specifically plan for our children to grow up seeing their parents enjoying life and investing time into their lives. As we have raised our children, we desperately wanted to enjoy them and have a lot of laughs along the way.

Chapter 11
Prayer

A Well-Kept Secret

"We will see an explosion of God's presence as a result of the prayers of His people."
- Dr. Tony Evans

People like to be in on secrets. Most people enjoy knowing something that others do not. Most folks will tell you quickly that they can be trusted to keep a secret. However, that is not what generally happens. Often, those who are told secrets cannot keep that the secret to themselves. There is an area of our spiritual life that I cannot wait to tell you more about.

One of the most underutilized spiritual privileges available to all believers is prayer. If I did not know better, I would think that the power and privilege of prayer is a well-kept secret because so few really utilize it in their daily lives. However, God never intended for us not to know about prayer and its power for living.

In fact, prayer is not optional for the believer. Look below at these verses to better understand this:

1) <u>It is an act of devotion.</u>
   "Devote yourselves to prayer, keeping alert in it with an attitude of thanksgiving; "Col 4:2 Everyone is devoted to something, most of us are devoted to more than one thing. When we choose to make something a priority we are willing to sacrifice for it. When you freely give your time to something you are devoted to it.

2) *It is a continual act*
   "pray without ceasing; "1 Thess 5:17
   Prayer is a relationship. Praying without ceasing is like communicating with God on one line while also taking calls on another.

3) *It is an act of necessity*
   "But He Himself would often slip away to the wilderness and pray." Luke 5:16
   If Christ, God incarnate, found it necessary to often slip away and pray, how much more necessary is it for us to follow His example.

I am convinced that it is time for Christians everywhere to understand the command, the obligation, and priority to pray. It is time for us to get in the battle for our families, our kids, our church, and this culture by getting on our knees and calling out to God.

Most of the great movements of God can be traced to a small group of praying people! For example, the last great awakening in this country occurred between the years 1857-1859. History tells us that this revival began with prayer. In New York, a businessman by the name of Jeremiah Lanphier started a small prayer group that met daily. It did not take long for this small group to begin to grow. Within a short time, almost 10,000 people would meet daily to pray for revival.

Indeed, spending time with God is life changing for an individual and for a corporate body of believers. Would you join our staff here at Metrolina in praying for our students, staff, and families as never before? Prayer was never intended to be a well-kept secret but instead God's design was for it to be our most treasured spiritual discipline.

Vital Signs

"To be a Christian without prayer is no more possible than to be alive without breathing."
Martin Luther

In just about every hospital room in America, there is a monitor above the bed that displays the patients' vital signs. The vital signs monitored are usually heart rate, oxygen levels, and blood pressure to name a few. These signs provide the doctors with an idea of how the patient is doing in the most critical areas such as our breathing and items related to our heart.

In our spiritual lives, we need to keep an eye on some of the vital areas of our lives that indicate what our Christian walk really looks like. One of those vital areas is that of our prayer life. Are we spending time with God in prayer building that relationship? Do we really know how to pray so that we can have an effective prayer life? We cannot grow our prayer life unless we really know how to approach God in prayer. I believe the best way to learn how to pray is to follow the model of Jesus. How did Jesus pray?

He prayed before making major decisions
It was at this time that He went off to the mountain to pray, and He spent the whole night in prayer to God. Luke 6:12. (Prior to choosing the twelve disciples)

He prayed after great victories
After He had sent the crowds away, He went up on the mountain by Himself to pray; and when it was evening, He was there alone. Matt 14:23. (After the feeding of the 5,000.)

He prayed to overcome temptation
And He came out and proceeded as was His custom to the Mount of Olives; and the disciples also followed Him. When He arrived at the place, He said to them, "Pray that you may not enter into temptation." Luke 22:39-41

He prayed with the right motive
Now, Father, glorify me together with Yourself, with the glory which I had with You before the world was. John 17:5

He prayed for intimacy with God.
This is eternal life that they may know You, the only true God, and Jesus Christ whom you have sent. John 17:3

He prayed scripture
Sanctify them in the truth; Your word is truth. John 17:17

He prayed during a crisis
When the sixth hour came, darkness fell over the whole land until the ninth hour. At the ninth hour Jesus cried out with a loud voice, "MY GOD, MY GOD, WHY HAVE YOU FORSAKEN ME?" Mark 15:33-34

He prayed to impact the world
I do not ask You to take them out of the world, but to keep them from the evil one. John 17:15

I pray that the model of Jesus will help you as you pray but I also want to leave you with another simple formula for prayer and it is called the ACTS model. ACTS stands for adoration, confession, thanksgiving, and supplication. Begin your prayers with praise for God, followed by any sins you need to confess, then express your thanks for all He has done for you, and finally make known your requests to God in the manner that Jesus did above.

May each of us begin to experience the true power of prayer!

Enemies of Prayer

Prayer is such a vital part of a growing relationship with God. Prayer changes our focus, our attitude, and our pursuits. James 5: 16 says that ***"the earnest prayer of a righteous person has great power and produces wonderful results."*** For this reason, I am convinced that the devil will do anything he can to distract us from having an effective and powerful prayer life.

The Bible provides us some insight as to what some of the enemies of prayer are that can keep us from prayer life that produces wonderful results. Below are some of those enemies:

Wrong Reasons
You ask and do not receive, because you ask with wrong motives, so that you may spend it on your pleasures.
James 4:3

Unconfessed Sin
If I regard wickedness in my heart, The Lord will not hear;
Psalms 66:18

A closed Bible
He who turns away his ear from listening to the law,
Even his prayer is an abomination.
Prov 28:9

Unbelief
"But he must ask in faith without any doubting, for the one who doubts is like the surf of the sea, driven and tossed by the wind. For that man ought not to expect that he will receive anything from the Lord."
James 1:6-7

Idols
"Son of man, these men have set up their idols in their hearts and have put right before their faces the stumbling block of their iniquity."
Ezekiel 14:3

Hypocrisy

"When you pray, you are not to be like the hypocrites; for they love to stand and pray in the synagogues and on the street corners so that they may be seen by men. Truly I say to you, they have their reward in full."
Matt 6:5

Unforgiveness

"Whenever you stand praying, forgive, if you have anything against anyone, so that your Father who is in heaven will also forgive you your transgressions."
Mark 11:25

Unresolved Conflict

"In the same way, you husbands must give honor to your wives. Treat your wife with understanding as you live together. She may be weaker than you are, but she is your equal partner in God's gift of new life. Treat her as you should so your prayers will not be hindered."
1 Peter 3:1-7

Unprayed prayers

"You lust and do not have; so you commit murder. You are envious and cannot obtain; so you fight and quarrel. You do not have because you do not ask."
James 4:2

I pray these verses will help as you pray and seek the heart of God. I am convinced that the spiritual discipline of prayer can change our lives. As we grow closer to God, we will even begin to pray as the Psalmist describes in Psalm 37:4 when he says: **"Take delight in the Lord, and he will give you your heart's desires."**

In other words, when we get consumed with God then we will begin to pray for things that will bring Him glory. At that point, we will begin to see God do things that would be beyond our imagination.

Essentials to an Effective Prayer Life

Prayer is one of the greatest privileges that we have as followers of Jesus Christ. However, it is also one of the least utilized and most misunderstood gifts for believers. James 4:3 describes this issue well when it says:

"And even when you ask, you don't get it because your motives are all wrong—you want only what will give you pleasure."

I love the way James phrases the issue of prayer when it says, **"even when you ask."** The sad part is that many times it is not our first thought to go to God with the issues of life but rather to attempt to fix it on our own. Next, he says that we many times we ask out of the wrong motives.

So then, how do we effectively get our prayers answered? Let me give you some Biblical principles for an effective prayer life.

1) <u>Ask in faith- James 1:6</u>
   "But when you ask him, be sure that your faith is in God alone. Do not waver, for a person with divided loyalty is as unsettled as a wave of the sea that is blown and tossed by the wind."
   We must believe that God is able to do what is needed and to trust Him for what is best.

2) <u>Pray in Jesus's name- John 16:24</u>
   "You haven't done this before. Ask, using my name, and you will receive, and you will have abundant joy."
   We should always ask in the name of Jesus. When we start asking that way, our motives will change.

3) <u>Pray according to God's will- 1 John 5:14</u>
   "And we are confident that he hears us whenever we ask for anything that pleases him."

We must allow God to change our hearts to the point that our focus will be on things that please Him and those prayers He will answer.

4) <u>**We must be in right relationship with others- 1 Peter 3:7**</u>
"In the same way, you husbands must give honor to your wives. Treat your wife with understanding as you live together. She may be weaker than you are, but she is your equal partner in God's gift of new life. Treat her as you should so your prayers will not be hindered."
We must be right with others to have an effective prayer life.

5) <u>**We cannot have unconfessed sin- Psalm 66:18**</u>
"If I had not confessed the sin in my heart, the Lord would not have listened."
These principles are essential to an effective prayer life. I pray that each of us would grow our prayer lives and our relationship with the Lord as never before.

<u>Sometimes Things Are Not As Easy As They Sound</u>

"Your will be done on earth as it is in Heaven. "Matthew 6:10

The Lord's Prayer is something we have all heard and said countless times. I am afraid that it has become so commonplace that we do not take the time to consider the significance of what we are praying. One of those easy to overlook verses in the Lord's Prayer is found in Matthew 6:10.

In this verse, we are asking that God's will be done on earth as it is in heaven. The obvious question then is how His will is done in Heaven. It is always done in Heaven and done immediately. Not only is it done immediately it is also completed joyfully.

Unfortunately, God's will is not done as often here on earth. We need to look no further than the daily news to see this fact. God's will is that all would be saved and follow Him completely but we clearly know that is not happening in our world.

Let's stop for a moment and consider the significance of praying Matthew 6:10. First, God does have a plan for our lives and that plan according to Romans 8:29 is that "we might be conformed to His image." In other words, we might grow daily to be more like Jesus. His will is for us to follow this path.

The problem is that so often His will conflicts with what we have on our agenda. We have a plan in our minds of what we want to accomplish with our lives. The question becomes whether our plan lines up with God's plan. When we pray Matthew 6:10, we are asking God to override our plans and our will for our lives. We are telling God that He wins. We are giving up what we believe best for our lives and truly trusting Him with our future.

Even though we have recited the Lord's Prayer thousands of times, Matthew 6:10 is not a casual prayer. It is a prayer of determination and intensity in which we readily admit that we want what God wants for our lives. I am convinced that this prayer is a very difficult prayer to pray.

I prayed this prayer many years ago and then God totally changed the direction of my career and life pursuits. That change has been difficult at times, but I can tell you without hesitation that is has also been the biggest blessing of my life. When we give God control of our lives, He can be trusted to do what is best for us!

I pray that the words of the Matthew 6:10 will come alive in all of our hearts. That we will daily submit to God's will for our lives. Psalm 37:4 declares: "Delight yourself in the Lord and He will give you the desires of your heart." This verse tells us that when His desires become our desires then He will truly give us His best for our lives.

Chapter 12
The Power of the Word

What's It Worth to You?

"So shall my word be that goes forth out of my mouth: it shall not return unto me void, but it shall accomplish that which I please, and it shall prosper in the thing whereto I sent it."
Isaiah 55:11

A lot of times in life when people ask us to do a favor for them we will jokingly use the phrase "What's it worth to you? The idea here being that if I do what you are asking is will be worth my time and trouble. In other words, it will benefit me to do whatever you are asking.

As Christians, we have been taught in church and read in the Bible that we are to discipline ourselves to study and memorize God's Word. Unfortunately, not many people in our culture spend time in the Word nor memorize it. The busyness and demands of life keeps us from following what God would have us to do. The key question then is what we are missing from not reading and memorizing God's Word.

What is it worth to us to study and memorize Scripture? Isaiah 55:11 tells us that His Word will accomplish great things in our life. This verse tells us that His Word is something that change who we are and more importantly prosper us spiritually. Even more than that, let me give you some specific ways that memorizing Scripture will bless you.

Memorizing Scripture will:

<u>Supply Spiritual Power</u>

"Thy word I have treasured in my heart that I may not sin against Thee." Psalms 119:11 His Word in our hearts will give us the tools to see sin coming and avoid it!

Strengthens Your Faith
*"Incline your ear and hear the words of the wise, and apply your mind to my knowledge; for it will be pleasant if you keep them within you, that they may be ready on your lips. So that your trust may be in the L*ORD*, I have taught you today, even you." Proverbs 22:17-19* God's Words will be available to you when you need it so that you may see your faith grow.

Prepares You to Witness
"But you will receive power when the Holy Spirit comes upon you. And you will be my witnesses, telling people about me everywhere—in Jerusalem, throughout Judea, in Samaria, and to the ends of the earth." Acts 1:8 As you and I are filled with His Word and His Spirit we will begin to experience the boldness and desire to tell others of His marvelous grace.

Provides Counsel
"Thy testimonies also are my delight; they are my counselors. "Psalms 119:24 Memorizing His Word will provide great counsel as we navigate the trials and daily demands of life.

Stimulates Meditation
"O how I love Thy law! It is my meditation all the day." Psalms 119:97 Memorizing God's Word will cause us to begin to meditate upon His truths which will change our hearts and our lives.

The reasons above are why we value teaching our students to memorize Scripture. I pray that we will all see the value of studying and memorizing God's Word. As you can see, it will accomplish much!

More than Words

"But prove yourselves doers of the word, and not merely hearers who delude themselves. For if anyone is a hearer of the word and not a doer, he is like a man who looks at his natural face in a mirror; for once he has looked at himself and gone away, he has immediately forgotten what kind of person he was. But one who looks intently at the perfect law, the law of liberty, and abides by it, not having become a forgetful hearer but an effectual doer, this man shall be blessed in what he does."
James 1:22-25

I have heard people describe some folks as "all talk and no action." As a follower of Jesus Christ, that is the last thing that I would ever want said about me. I want to as James 1 declares to be not only a hearer of the Word but also a doer. How then do we take what the Word of God tells us and apply it to our lives?

There are a lot of Bible study plans out there that will help us navigate our way through the Scriptures. What should we be looking for as we study the Bible that we can practically use in our everyday life? I want to provide you with six application questions to use as a guide when you study the Bible.

1) Does this text reveal something about the nature of God?
2) Does this text reveal something I should praise, thank or trust God for?
3) Does this text reveal something I should pray for, for me or others?
4) Does this text reveal something that I should have a new attitude about?
5) Does this text reveal something I should make a decision about?
6) Does this text reveal something I should do for Christ, others or myself?

From these questions, we can look next for specific applications for our lives. These specific applications are:

1) **Is there a sin to confess?**
2) **Is there a promise to claim?**
3) **Is there an example to follow?**
4) **Is there a command to obey?**
5) **Is there an idea about God to know?**
6) **Is there an error to avoid?**
7) **Is there someone to pray for?**

My desire is that I will be effective in obeying God's Word and living out the Christian life from a Biblical Worldview. When we make the everyday decisions of life whether big or small according to the Bible we are in essence living with a Biblical Worldview. I pray that our lives will be more than just words.

Chapter 13
Real Commitment

An Unusual Attitude

"Finally, dear brothers and sisters, we urge you in the name of the Lord Jesus to live in a way that pleases God, as we have taught you. You live this way already, and we encourage you to excel still more."
1 Thessalonians 4:1

My mom and dad taught me so much growing up. As I look back, I cherish all those things that I learned. Especially, how they taught me to love God with all ***"my, heart, soul, and mind."*** However, one overriding principle that they taught has helped guide me all these years.

This principle is one that they encouraged me to apply to everything I did. They taught me to do everything I did in life with 100% effort and determination so that I might always get better and never be satisfied with where I am at in life.

The attitude of wanting to get better, improve, and go beyond the call of duty is an unusual attitude today as we live in a culture that many times encourages us to do only what's necessary to get by.

The Apostle Paul in 1 Thessalonians 4:1 sends us the exact same message when he tells us ***"to excel still more."*** He is essentially reminding us to never be satisfied and to continue to live in a way each day that ***"pleases God."***

So then, how can we live in a way that pleases God and that allows us to *"excel still more?"* These are some ways God has reminded me of in HIs Word:

1) <u>**A Complete Commitment to Him**</u>
   We prioritize those relationships that are most important to us. We should continually examine our lives to see where we are spending our time, with whom, and on what in comparison to what we offer the Lord.
   "You must love the LORD your God with all your heart, all your soul, and all your mind." Matthew 22:37

2) <u>*A Worthy Commitment*</u>
   Most of the time eating leftovers are never as good as they when were first prepared. Giving God our leftover time, treasure, and talent are not going to allow us to grow and excel as a believer. He deserves our best and as David says it ought to cost us something.
   "I will not present burnt offerings that have cost me nothing!" 1Chronicles 21:24

3) *An Attitude of Excellence*
   I want to have an attitude that fixes *"my thoughts"* on the things of God. I want to focus my effort what is excellent in God's eyes and things that will be worthy of praise to Him.
   "And now, dear brothers and sisters, one final thing. Fix your thoughts on what is true, and honorable, and right, and pure, and lovely, and admirable. Think about things that are excellent and worthy of praise." Philippians 4:8

My prayer is that these unusual attitudes would permeate the lives of our students, staff, and our entire school!

What Real Sacrifice Looks Like!

"Since he did not spare even his own Son but gave him up for us all, won't he also give us everything else?"
Romans 8:32

My parents sacrificed a lot in life to take care of me and provide for me as I was growing up. My problem was that I did not fully appreciate it until I was grown up. I am not sure that I even understand the depth of love that real sacrifice requires until I became an adult.

One of Webster's definitions of sacrifice is the **"destruction or surrender of something for the sake of something else".** My parents surrendered a lot of their wants and aspirations to provide for me. All because of the unconditional love that they had for me.

My parent's sacrifices were great, but nothing compared to what God has provided for us. Romans 8:32 above so powerfully tells us what real sacrifice looks like. God **"did not spare His own Son but gave Him up for us all."** God sacrificed what was most precious to Him for you and me.

He did that to not only pay the penalty for our sins and give us eternal life but also that we might have **"life and have it more abundantly"** as John 10:10 describes. I love also the last phrase of Romans 8:32 which says, **"won't He also give us everything else?"**

He stands ready to give us joy, peace, love, and all things that pertain to life. He sacrificed His Son, so He could do those things for us. This is what real sacrifice looks like. God is **"All In"** for us! Stop and think about the idea that the great God of this universe gave it all for you and me!

Maybe today you are discouraged and beaten down. Allow the truth of Romans 8:32 to touch your heart today and remind you that you are a child of the King and He wants to give you the help you need today to live the life He has planned for you.

As we are reminded of the great truth from Romans 8:32, I pray we will also be challenged because of our love for God to be **"All In"** for Him. Christianity has shrunk in its influence in recent years according to research. I believe mainly because our commitment and sacrifice as Christians to God has waned.

If those of us who claim the name of Christ would live **"All In"** for God more consistently, then I believe we could shake this world for Christ in ways we would never imagine!

My heart's desire is that we as individuals and the community of Metrolina would commit ourselves to loving and living for God. What we would gain in this world and the next would be far greater than any sacrifice we could give!

Recognizing and Chasing Real Treasure

"We now have this light shining in our hearts, but we ourselves are like fragile clay jars containing this great treasure. This makes it clear that our great power is from God, not from ourselves."
2 Corinthians 4:7

Treasure hunting has long been the fascination of so many in our society. Searching for lost treasure is the ultimate get rich quick scheme. The fascination of lost treasure has even resulted in the making of two blockbuster movies called ***"National Treasure."*** In the end, none of this so-called treasure really satisfies.

How do I know that simply acquiring treasure will not satisfy? You need look no further than King Solomon. Ecclesiastes 2 tells us that Solomon acquired more earthly treasure than anyone in history and yet it did not satisfy him. Verse eleven of Chapter 2 records Solomon's thoughts on earthly treasure.

> ***"But as I looked at everything I had worked so hard to accomplish, it was all so meaningless—like chasing the wind. There was nothing really worthwhile anywhere."***

Solomon says all this worldly treasure is meaningless and not worthwhile. I am afraid that so many people will spend their lives working hard chasing the American dream and acquiring stuff only to realize the truth of what Solomon is saying.

Instead of pursuing worldly treasure, Paul reminds us in 2 Corinthians 4:7 of the real treasure that we as believers have in Christ. Paul reminds us that when we are saved that God puts a ***"light shining in our heart."*** Even with this light, we still occupy our earthly bodies where we will face struggles and hardships. However, because of our relationship with Jesus we have this incredible light of hope that supersedes all our difficulties.

Paul goes on to tell us that this light is a ***"great treasure"*** that we have within us. This is a real treasure that has ***"great power"*** for us to live this life. This is a treasure that will not fade away or be meaningless. This is a treasure that we will have not only in this lifetime but also throughout eternity. There is no substitute for the light, the hope, and the peace that the treasure of God provides for us.

Maybe it is about time that we remind ourselves as Christians that this world is not really our home. As well, the things of this world will never satisfy. I love how C.S. Lewis put this thought years ago, when he said: ***"If I find in myself a desire which no experience in this world can satisfy, the most probable explanation is that I was made for another world."***

I pray that these verses will encourage your heart and remind you of the ***"great treasure"*** that God has placed in us!

Committed to Making a Difference

"When you encourage others, you in the process are encouraged because you're making a commitment and difference in that person's life. Encouragement really does make a difference."
Zig Ziglar

I will never forget one of my ninth-grade teachers by the name of Mr. Fellers. Mr. Fellers worked so hard in my life to encourage me to do my best and he always reminded me of how much potential I had if I only applied myself. Mr. Fellers was committed to making a difference in the lives of students as an educator. I am so grateful for the difference he made in my life.

What about us? Are we making a difference in the lives of others? What are we committed to? It is easy in the hustle and bustle of this life to get so busy and so focused on what we are doing that we lose sight of the difference we can make in the lives of others.

I was reminded of this recently when I was doing my morning devotion and read Philippians 2:1. That verse pricked my heart when I read the words of Paul when he said:

"Is there any encouragement from belonging to Christ? Any comfort from his love? Any fellowship together in the Spirit? Are your hearts tender and compassionate?"

I began to think of my own life and testimony and wondered if my heart was tender and compassionate towards others as it should be. God used that verse to remind me of just how good that God has been to me. I recognized that clearly when I read the words *"Is there any encouragement from belonging to Christ"?*

I was reminded afresh and anew of how God has saved me and encouraged me over the years. Oh, how He has comforted me with

His love at times when I thought my world was falling apart. This verse challenged me to make sure that my heart is committed or ***"All In"*** in being tender and compassionate towards others.

I pray that the community of Metrolina may be known as a place that is tender and compassionate towards others. I pray that we may use God's Word to bring hope and encouragement to all those around us.

I love how the Apostle Paul reminded us in Romans 15:4 of the power of God's Word when he said:

> ***"Such things were written in the Scriptures long ago to teach us. And the Scriptures give us hope and encouragement as we wait patiently for God's promises to be fulfilled."***

May we be committed to giving others hope and encouragement through God's Word as we wait for His promises to be fulfilled!

Talk is Cheap

> ***"For the Kingdom of God is not just a lot of talk; it is living by God's power.***
> ***"1 Corinthians 4:20***

Christianity Today has conducted recent research that indicates almost 78% of all Americans identify themselves as Christian. If that is true, then why is church attendance in decline in this country? Also, why do so many people struggle living with a Biblical worldview or in other words making their everyday decisions of life according to God's Word?

I am sure you have heard the old saying that goes like this: **"You can talk the talk but are you walking the walk?"** I am afraid that many people are living very defeated and discouraged Christian lives because they are not living their daily lives with God's power. Many I believe are talking about Kingdom living but struggle with really this principle out.

How can we live out the idea of operating our lives under the power of our great God? To begin with, we must daily commit our wills to His. To do this, we must spend time with Him daily by studying the Bible and also spending time with Him in prayer. With that as a starting point, we must then begin to daily give God control of our lives and our desires. Specifically, we must commit ourselves to living out the truth of Galatians 2:20. That verse declares:

> *"My old self has been crucified with Christ. It is no longer I who live, but Christ lives in me. So I live in this earthly body by trusting in the Son of God, who loved me and gave himself for me."*

What does this look like in everyday life? Simply, to pray daily for God to live through you in every decision and action you take. My desire for my life is that each day I pray and ask God for His wisdom and discernment in all that I do. As Galatians 2:20 tells us, we must begin to trust Him for every detail of life. The Bible has clear principles for all that we will encounter in life. Not only does it provide principles for living, but it also provides the power we need for living these principles out.

I love the promise that is contained in Philippians 2:13.

> *"For God is working in you, giving you the desire and the power to do what pleases him."*

I do not want my Christian life to be all talk. I do not want others to see me as a hypocrite. I want others to see the power of God operating in my life daily. Philippians 2:13 offers us the hope that God is working in our lives and giving us the power, we need to walk the walk. This verse gives us the hope that we do not have to live defeated or discouraged Christian lives.

I pray for those who are defeated or discouraged today that you may be encouraged by the truth of Philippians 2:13. I pray that each of us will see the power of God come alive in our lives so that our Christian lives will be more than just talk.

Understanding Who Is Responsible for What

"Yes, I am the vine; you are the branches. Those who remain in me, and I in them, will produce much fruit. For apart from me you can do nothing."
John 15:5

During my work career, I have always wanted to know exactly what I was responsible for doing and who my boss was and their expectations. I think like to know upfront who is responsible for what. Unfortunately, many times people confuse those roles. Conflict and stress are inevitable when someone tries to do things that are not theirs to do.

The same thing can happen to us in our spiritual lives. We begin to get this idea at times that we are responsible for doing great things for the Kingdom on our own. John 15:5 makes it clear that this was never God's plan for us.

In that verse, Jesus tells us that that He is the Vine and we are the branches. It is interesting that He uses this analogy of a plant or tree. The vine is part of the tree that provides the nutrients and ingredients necessary to produce fruit. The branches simply bear the fruit.

What Jesus is telling us here is that He alone produces the fruit in our lives. As much as we try, we cannot produce fruit like love, joy, and peace in our lives that will last apart from Him. What then are we responsible for? We are responsible for staying in close relationship to Him.

With John 15:5 in mind, our responsibility is to abide in Him. What exactly does that mean? The idea of the vine here is that we must be connected to Him to receive the things necessary for us to produce fruit in our lives. Not only must we maintain the connection, we are also dependent on the vine for our direction, our hope, and our path forward. Also, we must continue or abide in Him for us to stay fruitful for the Kingdom.

All of this is reminding us who is responsible for what. We are not responsible for producing fruit. We are responsible for abiding in Him. This means that we are to no longer pursue our agenda for our lives but instead commit the control of our lives to Him. To do this, we must daily cultivate our relationship with Him through prayer and study of His Word.

I love how Frances Chan described this idea when he said:

"There are periods that we forget that in the pursuit of fruit, that if we just abide in Him, then fruitfulness is a guarantee."

May we all find comfort in knowing that Jesus will do in our lives what only He can do if we remain in Him. Because ***"apart from Him we can do nothing."***

I Am Fixing To

"You will keep in perfect peace all who trust in you, all whose thoughts are fixed on you!"
Isaiah 26:3

Sometimes we Southerners use expressions that people outside the South do not understand. One of those phrases we use some sometimes is the phrase *"I am fixing to."* Translated it means that we are getting ready or prepared to do something.

In this crazy world we live in, I want to do all I can to be ready spiritually for all the issues of life that will come my way. I am convinced that if we are not ready spiritually we will miss out on the peace we all so desperately seek for our lives. I want to be focused and fixated on Him daily.

Isaiah 26:3 above gives us an incredible prescription for finding peace for our lives. In this passage, Isaiah tells us that God will keep *"in perfect peace"* all those who trust in Him and who are focused or fixated on Him.

As I thought about this idea of placing our trust in God, that is what we as Christians did when we received Christ as Savior and Lord. At that time, He secured our eternal destiny. This is the first step of gaining peace with God as the verse above says. We are secure in Him for eternity. Hebrews 9:12 describes this:

> *"With his own blood—not the blood of goats and calves—he entered the Most Holy Place once for all time and <u>secured our redemption forever.</u>"*

We are secure in Him and that should bring us peace. The second part of gaining that peace is in being fixated or focused on Him. I researched the definition of fixed. Webster defines it as *"securely placed or fastened."* Once we are saved and in relationship with God, we are to daily place our hope and trust in Him for all the issues of life. He is our anchor that will hold our lives calm and steady regardless of whatever the storms of life may bring us.

Hebrews 6:18-19 confirms this when it declares:

> *"Therefore, we who have fled to him for refuge can have great confidence as we hold to the hope that lies before us.*

> *This hope is a strong and trustworthy anchor for our souls.*
> *It leads us through the curtain into God's inner sanctuary."*
> **Hebrews 6:18-19**

He is the only hope that can truly bring us peace. The primary thing we should be **"fixing to do"** as the Southern expression says is to allow our thoughts, our lives, and our hopes to be fixed on God!

Someday You Will

> *"Jesus replied, "You don't understand now*
> *what I am doing, but someday you will."*
> **John 13:7**

Growing up, I heard my mom say many times to me that you do not understand what is going on now but someday you will. At the time, that statement never made sense to me as a child. I wanted to know now why something was happening.

Even today, I think we all struggle with why certain things happen to us or people we know. Life does not make sense many times whether it be in trying to find a career path or trying to understand why a loved one has been diagnosed with a terminal illness.

In John 13:7, Jesus tells us that even though *"you don't understand now what I am doing, but someday you will."* What a great truth and reminder! In Isaiah 55:8, God reminds us *"My thoughts are not your thoughts, nor are your ways My ways."*

These verses teach us that God is at work in our lives many times behind the scenes and in a way that is far superior to anything we could think of. I am living proof that God's plan is a lot whole lot better than mine. When I was fresh out of college, I really believed that my career path would solely be about finding the right business career.

It was not long that I was miserable in those business jobs. I began to pray and ask God why do you have me here? Answers did not come right away, and it appears I was trapped in something I hated. When I look back on those times, I see now that it was as if God was telling me to hang on and learn all I could where He had me and that someday soon He would reveal to me His plan.

That was exactly what He did. He used business experience in my life to help prepare me for the role to lead Metrolina. I did not have to wait to long for the Lord to give me that "someday." He planted me in a role that I went back to school for and used those earlier tools in business to make a difference in ministry. I did not know then, but I gained an understanding of what God was up to all these years later.

What about you? Maybe you are in a place today that you don't why something is happening in your life. I would remind you that God has His best planned for you if you will trust Him. Especially if you will trust Him to deliver you in His own unique way. I want to leave you with some verses that I pray will give you hope that someday you will understand.

> *"The Lord your God walks in the midst*
> *of your camp, to deliver you."*
> *Deuteronomy 23:14*

> *"The righteous person faces many troubles, but*
> *the* Lord *comes to the rescue each time."*
> *Psalm 34:19*

Chapter 14
Struggles We All Face

A Familiar Problem

"For my people have done two evil things: They have abandoned Me—the fountain of living water. And they have dug for themselves cracked cisterns that can hold no water at all!"
-Jeremiah 2:13

People have searched throughout history to find real meaning to life and happiness. This search for significance has led people in so many different directions. Most of these pursuits whether it be money, fame, self-accomplishment, a relationship, or anything that this world has to offer will leave you without real meaning or a lasting hope.

As believers, we also get caught in chasing the wrong things. In Jeremiah 2:13, this age old basic problem is best described. This verse tells us that many times we make two bad choices. First, we do not go to God or rely on Him for all aspects of our lives. The second bad decision we make is that instead of relying on God we choose to rely on something or someone of this world that cannot help us at all.

What is worse is that many times we keep making these mistakes over and over. I know personally of many times in my own life where I have continued over and over to fix the issues of my life with the world's solutions. At those times, I can tell you that I have never been more personally frustrated.

Albert Einstein made famous the quote that **"Insanity is: doing the same thing over and over again and expecting different results."**

When we continually abandon God for solutions that *"cannot hold water"* it is, as Einstein says, somewhat insane.

Jeremiah tells us that God is the *"fountain of living water"* who alone can meet our needs and help us discover real meaning and purpose for our lives. I do not want to live my life dealing with this same old problem that Jeremiah described. Solutions that *"cannot hold water"* have only left me empty, worn out, and frustrated.

Instead, I want to live my life drinking daily from the *"fountain of living water."* My prayer is that God would use Jeremiah 2:13 to refresh your soul and remind you that our real source of hope rests only in a daily, growing relationship with God.

What Are You Living Up To?

"In any case, we should live to whatever truth we have attained.

Dear brothers and sisters, pattern your lives after mine, and learn from those who follow our example. For I have told you often before, and I say it again with tears in my eyes, that there are many whose conduct shows they are really enemies of the cross of Christ."
Philippians 3:16-18

I think we all at times have looked for models to pattern our lives after. I was fortunate to grow up in a home where my dad was someone who I could pattern my life after spiritually. He was a man who loved God, loved God's Word, and loved me.

One of my biggest fears about being a parent was that I could be the type of role model that my children could pattern their lives after. My heart's desire has long been that my children would see Jesus in me. I sought God for a long time for answers on how to live up to this desire. God has given me Philippians 3:16-20 as my answer for doing this.

In this passage, Paul made an incredible statement above when he asked those around him to *"pattern their lives after his and follow those who follow our example."* I do not believe that Paul had an attitude of arrogance in believing that he had arrived spiritually. I know that because in Philippians 3:12 he declares *"that I have not arrived."*

So, how does he make that kind of statement? I believe it comes not from confidence in himself but confidence in what God had done in his life. Paul had once been an enemy of the cross as he describes in verse 18. What did Paul mean by the statement *"an enemy of the cross"*?

Verse 19 of Philippians 3 gives us that answer when it says: *"They are headed for destruction. Their god is their appetite, they brag about shameful things, and they think only about this life here on earth."* Paul knew that he had been rescued from a life that was headed in the wrong direction and only focused on the things of this world.

Instead, Paul had experienced the truth of verse 20 in this chapter and had committed his life to the truth of this verse. Verse 20 declares: *"But we are citizens of heaven, where the Lord Jesus Christ lives. And we are eagerly waiting for Him to return as our Savior."* Everything about Paul's focus and direction for living had changed.

He was no longer focused on the things of this world but instead he operated his lifestyle from the vantage point of a citizen of Heaven. Paul's quest now was to live for Jesus and to do so in such a way that God would be glorified. Paul had seen the difference in his own life that Jesus makes. From the confidence he now had in Christ, he could tell others to follow or pattern their lives after what God had done in his life.

Paul had decided to live up to the standards required of a citizen of Heaven. I knew that for me to give my kids a pattern that they could follow I would have to allow God to change my vantage point. I would need to focus on growing my relationship with Christ and allowing

Him to give me the mindset of a citizen of Heaven. I learned that I must be living in such a way as to bring honor and glory to God in all I do.

I pray that we all would seek to live up to what God has called us to!

The Mirror Does Not Lie

"For if you listen to the word and don't obey, it is like glancing at your face in a mirror. You see yourself, walk away, and forget what you look like. But if you look carefully into the perfect law that sets you free, and if you do what it says and don't forget what you heard, then God will bless you for doing it."
James 1:23-25

As I have gotten older, I sometimes think in my mind that I am still a young man. In those times, I find it hard to believe that I have gotten old. However, one look in the mirror reminds me of the truth. The mirror reveals the gray hair and wrinkles that are there dispelling the notion that I am still a young man.

Once I have seen what the mirror reveals, I can choose to walk away content with what I have seen or I can choose to make a change to my appearance. I could choose plastic surgery to remove wrinkles or dye my hair to change my appearance, so I can have the mirror reflect something different in the future. (No need to worry-I am not doing that). My point is the mirror just reflects what is there.

In the passage above, James shares a similar analogy about the mirror when it comes to our spiritual lives. He tells us that reading and hearing the Word of God will reveal who we really are and the true condition of our walk with God. The passage speaks of how we many times will see the picture of who we are through God's Word, but we will walk away quickly without making any changes to our lives.

Other times, I am afraid we will not even consider the mirror of God's truth because we do not want to face what the mirror of truth will tell us. I know that this has been true in my life at times in the past. When we do this, we are being held captive to a life that never satisfies.

This passage in James is offering us a better way to approach the mirror of truth. Instead of looking and quickly walking away from it, he is instructing us to *"look carefully"* at the truth that *"sets you free"* and *"do what it says."*

James is teaching us to do three things. First, he is telling us to meditate on the Word of God, second to obey what it says, and lastly to not forget it. Let me leave you with two verses to consider that will help us as we approach the mirror of truth.

"Study this Book of Instruction continually. Meditate on it day and night so you will be sure to obey everything written in it. Only then will you prosper and succeed in all you do."
Joshua 1:8

"I have hidden your word in my heart, that I might not sin against you."
Psalm 119:11

The mirror truly does not lie! I pray that we would all look carefully at what God is revealing to us through His Word!

Sometimes Things Are Not as Easy as They Sound

"Your will be done on earth as it is in Heaven."
Matthew 6:10

The Lord's Prayer is something we have all heard and said countless times. I am afraid that it has become so commonplace that we do not take the time to consider the significance of what we are praying. One of those easy to overlook verses in the Lord's Prayer is found in Matthew 6:10.

In this verse, we are asking that God's will be done on earth as it is in heaven. The obvious question then is how His will is done in Heaven. It is always done in Heaven and done immediately. Not only is it done immediately it is also completed joyfully.

Unfortunately, God's will is not done as often here on earth. We need to look no further than the daily news to see this fact. God's will be that all would be saved and follow Him completely, but we clearly know that is not happening in our world.

Let's stop for a moment and consider the significance of praying Matthew 6:10. First, God does have a plan for our lives and that plan according to Romans 8:29 is that "we might be conformed to His image." In other words, we might grow daily to be more like Jesus. His will is for us to follow this path.

The problem is that so often His will conflicts with what we have on our agenda. We have a plan in our minds of what we want to accomplish with our lives. The question becomes whether our plan lines up with God's plan. When we pray Matthew 6:10, we are asking God to override our plans and our will for our lives. We are telling God that He wins. We are giving up what we believe best for our lives and truly trusting Him with our future.

Even though we have recited the Lord's Prayer thousands of times, Matthew 6:10 is not a casual prayer. It is a prayer of determination and intensity in which we readily admit that we want what God wants for our lives. I am convinced that this prayer is a very difficult prayer to pray.

I prayed this prayer many years ago and then God totally changed the direction of my career and life pursuits. That change has been difficult at times, but I can tell you without hesitation that is has also been the biggest blessing of my life. When we give God control of our lives, He can be trusted to do what is best for us!

I pray that the words of the Matthew 6:10 will come alive in all our hearts. That we will daily submit to God's will for our lives. Psalm 37:4 declares: "Delight yourself in the Lord and He will give you the desires of your heart." This verse tells us that when His desires become our desires then He will truly give us His best for our lives.

Are We Faithful Enough for God to Do Big Things in Our Life?

> "And He could do no mighty work, save that He laid His hands upon a few sick folk, and healed them. And He marveled because of their unbelief. And He went round about the villages teaching."
> Mark 6:5-6

Years ago, entertainer Art Linkletter was given the opportunity by Walt Disney to buy land that would become the home of Disneyland. Linkletter walked away from the deal because he considered the land a "wasteland" and the idea a little too risky. Today, the investment would be worth billions.

A lot of times in our Christian walk we are too hesitant about doing big bold things for God and stepping out in faith. I remember starting at Metrolina almost 17 years ago in a school of less than 200 students, not many staff members, and no real financing. I was scared to death and unsure about where God was leading. As I look back, I am grateful that I summoned enough courage to trust God and be a part of this great ministry. I never dreamed how He would bless it. If I had not trusted Him, I am confident that God would have used someone else to accomplish His purpose at Metrolina and I would have missed the blessing.

In Mark 6:5-6, Jesus makes a statement that gives me great pause when I think about the idea of having enough faith in Him to do what He has called us to do. Jesus says because of this people's unbelief that He could do no mighty work there. In fact, it says He was amazed at their unbelief.

I do not ever want my unbelief or lack of faith in God to keep Him from doing mighty things in my ministry or in my personal life. My prayer is that I will be sensitive to the doors that God opens for me in ministry and my personal life so that He can do a mighty work in my life.

Also, we need to be reminded that many times when these doors are opened that we will face opposition. The Apostle addressed this 1 Corinthians 16:9 when he declared: "For a great door and effectual is opened unto me, and there are many adversaries." May God not only grant us courage but also the wisdom to understand that we will face opposition when we follow Him completely.

Opportunities are going to come for all of us as believers to enter into a deeper commitment to Christ and as a result be presented with opportunities to do big bold things for the Kingdom. I hope that we will learn to trust God more than ever and allow Him to lead us through those doors for His glory. May it never be said of us that "He could do no mighty work" because of our unbelief!

Unsettled

"But when you ask him, be sure that your faith is in God alone. Do not waver, for a person with divided loyalty is as unsettled as a wave of sea that is blown and tossed by the wind. Such people should not expect to receive anything from the Lord. Their loyalty is divided between God and the world, and they are unstable in everything they do." James 1:6-8

A house or other structure that is built on unsettled ground, like sand, has a great chance to collapse. A house must be built on solid, settled ground such as rock for it to be able to stand up to all the elements of weather. Similarly, our spiritual lives must be built on solid ground so that we will not be unsettled in our thinking or living.

However, the world we live in today operates with a very dualistic mindset. What do I mean by dualism? Webster defines dualism as: "the quality or state of having two different or opposite parts or elements." What does this look like today in our world?

People live and behave one way in church and around Christians and then go off during the week with a different mindset that characterizes them in their workplace and other settings. For the most part, dualism describes a lifestyle that is compartmentalized depending on where we are and what we are doing.

God never intended for us to live this way. He never intended for us to be double-minded or unsettled. James 1:8 tells us that **"a double-minded man is unstable in everything he does."**

Being double-minded explains how I can see people on social media one day post a Bible verse and proclaim how God is their life and a day later curse and swear on that same social media sight. James 3:9-12 tells us that this lifestyle should not happen in the life of a believer.

"With it we bless our God and Father, and with it we curse men, who have been made in the similitude of God. Out of the same mouth proceed blessing and cursing. My brethren, these things ought not to be so. Does a spring send forth fresh water and bitter from the same opening? Can a fig tree, my brethren, bear olives, or a grapevine bear figs? Thus no spring yields both salt water and fresh."

Our goal must be to settle our faith and allegiance alone to the Lord Jesus Christ. We must integrate truth into every area of our life so that we can not only prevent a dualistic mindset but, more importantly, develop a Biblical worldview for ourselves and our family.

Living out a biblical worldview means that we will allow God to shape our thinking, our values, our actions, our behaviors and thus make all the decisions of life through the lens of God's Word. Establishing God's truth as the foundation for your life, your home, and raising your kids is fundamental to building your house on a rock.

As the old hymn says, "On Christ the solid rock I stand all other ground is sinking sand."

Endnotes

Chapter 1
1. Schultz, Dr. Glen. "Kingdom Education.for the 21st Century." 2011 Kingdom Education Ministries.www.KingdomEducation.org
2. Lewis, C.S. "C.S. Lewis Quotes." Famous Quotes and Quotations at BrainyQuote. Date unknown. November 2018. http://www.brainyquote.com/quotes/authors/c/c_s_lewis.html
3. Psalm 127:3-4
4. Psalm 78:4-7
5. Ephesians 5:33
6. Ephesians 5:25-26
7. 2 Corinthians 7:5
8. Ephesians 6:11-18
9. Proverbs 3:5-6
10. Luke 2:52
11. Luke 6:40
12. Colossians 2:8-9
13. Hebrews 12:11
14. Hebrews 5:16
15. Deuteronomy 12:8
16. Lewis, C.S. "C.S. Lewis Quotes." Famous Quotes and Quotations at BrainyQuote. Date unknown. November 2018. http://www.brainyquote.com/quotes/authors/c/c_s_lewis.html
17. Proverbs 22:6
18. Proverbs 29:7
19. Proverbs 4:23
20. Deuteronomy 6:7
21. 3 John 4
22. Ephesians 4:14

23. Psalm 63:1
24. Daniel 2:20-21
25. 1 Corinthians 4:20
26. Ephesians 6:10
27. Romans 12:2
28. Tozier, A.W. "A.W. Tozier Quotes. Popular Quotes at Goodreads. Date unknown. October 2018." http://www.goodreads.com/quotes/904965-complacency-is-a-deadly-foe-of-all-spiritual-growth
29. Graham, Billy. "Billy Graham Quote." http://www.brainyquote.com/searchresults.html?q=billy+Graham
30. Anonymous Quote. http://www.brainyquote.com/quotes/topics/topic dreams. Html
31. Fulgham, Robert. Robert Fulgham quotes at Brainy Quote. Date unknown. December 2018. https://www.brainyquote.com/search_results?q=robert+fulgham

Chapter 2

1. Romans 4:20-21
2. Jeremiah 31:3
3. Romans 8:37
4. 2 Peter 1:4
5. 1 Peter 1:23
6. 1 John 4:4
7. Proverbs 29:6
8. Matthew 5:3
9. 1 Corinthians 2:9
10. Matthew 5:8
11. 1 Samuel 15:22
12. 1 Peter 4:2
13. Philippians 3:7-8
14. Matthew 5:9
15. Matthew 5:6
16. Matthew 6:33

17. Lewis, C.S. "C.S. Lewis Quotes." Famous Quotes and Quotations at BrainyQuote. Date unknown. November 2018. http://www.brainyquote.com/quotes/authors/c/c_s_lewis.html

Chapter 3
1. 2 Timothy 1:9
2. Colossains 4:6
3. 1 Corinthians 9:24-26
4. John 8:32
5. Hebrews 12:15
6. Ephesians 2:8-9
7. 2 Corinthians 12:9-10
8. Ephesians 3:16-19
9. Deuteronomy 33:12
10. Romans 8:38
11. Deuteronomy 32:10
12. Romans 9:25
13. Psalm 46:10
14. 1 Kings 18:21
15. Deuteronomy 7:9
16. Tozier, A.W. "A.W. Tozier Quotes. Popular Quotes at Goodreads. Date unknown. October 2018. " http://www.goodreads.com/quotes/904965-complacency-is-a-deadly-foe-of-all-spiritual-growth
17. Washington, George. George Washington Quotes at Brainy quote. Date unknown. November 2018. https://www.brainyquote.com/authors/george_washington.
18. Lucado, Max. Max Lucado quotes at Brainy quote. Date unknown. November 2018. https://www.brainyquote.com/search_results?q=max+lucado
19. "Grace Greater than Our Sin." http://www.hymnsite.com/lyrics/umh365.sht

Chapter 4

1. Philippians 1:9-10
2. Psalm 122:1
3. Daniel 11:32
4. Nehemiah 8:10
5. 2 Thessalonians 3:12
6. Proverbs 22:4
7. Galatians 2:20
8. Proverbs 9:10
9. Luke 2:52
10. Luther, Martin. "Martin Luther Quotes." Famous Quotes and quotations at BrainyQuote. Date Unknown, December 2018.
11. Jefferson, Thomas. Thomas Jefferson quotes at Brainy Quote. Date unknown. December 2018. https://www.brainyquote.com/search_results?q=thomas+jefferson

Chapter 5

1. Ephesians 4:29
2. Philippians 2:3-4
3. Philippians 2:5-8
4. 1 Corinthians 2:5
5. Acts 5:25
6. 1 Timothy 3:17
7. Philippians 2:4
8. Hebrews 13:7
9. James 1:27
10. John 3:16
11. Psalm 115:1
12. Matthew 5:8
13. Genesis 22:12
14. Ephesians 6:12
15. Ephesians 4:15
16. 2 Peter 1:2-3
17. Colossians 2:3

18. Matthew 6:33
19. Ephesians 3:20
20. Psalm 37:4
21. Lamentations 3:23
22. 1 John 1:9
23. Whitson, Dr. Mike. "Dr. Mike Whitson Quote." Twitter. February 2015.
24. Franklin, Benjamin. Benjamin Franklin's quotes at Brainy Quote. Date unknown. December 2018. https://www.brainyquote.com/search_results?q=Benjamin+franklin.
25. Moody, D. L. D.L. Moody quotes at Brainy quote. Date unknown. December 2018. https://www.brainyquote.com/search_results?q=d.l.+moody
26. Oswald Chambers, "My Utmost for His Highest." (Uhrichsville, OH:Barbour,1963)
27. Ford, Henry. Henry Ford quotes at Brainy quote. Date unknown. December 2018. https://www.brainyquote.com/search_results?q=henry+ford

Chapter 6
1. 2 Corinthians 5:18-19
2. John 3:16
3. Colossians 3:13
4. Nahum 1:7
5. 2 Corinthians 12:9
6. Ephesians 1:19
7. Psalm 94:19
8. Philippians 4:19
9. John 16:33
10. Romans 8:18
11. Romans 12:14,17
12. 2 Corinthians 1:8
13. Lamentations 3:22
14. Isaiah 43:2

15. 2 Samuel 22:30
16. Matthew 28:20
17. Philippians 4:3
18. 2 Timothy 1:7
19. Ephesians 1:19-20
20. Moody, D. L. D.L. Moody quotes at Brainy quote. Date unknown. December 2018. https://www.brainyquote.com/search_results?q=d.l.+moody
21. Stanley, Charles. Charles Stanley quotes at Brainy quote. Date unknown. December 2018. https://www.brainyquote.com/search_results?q=stanley
22. Boom, Corrie Ten. "Corrie Ten Boom Quote. http://www.goodreads.com/author/quotes/102203.
23. Tada, Joni earickson. Joni Earickson Tada quotes at Brainy Quote. Date unknown. December 2018. https://www.brainyquote.com/search_results?q=joni+earickson+tada

Chapter 7
1. Proverbs 16:3
2. Joshua 1:8
3. Romans 10:17
4. Matthew 4:4
5. Ezra 7:10
6. Munroe, Myles. Myles Munroe quotes at Brainy quote. Date unknown. December 2018. https://www.brainyquote.com/search_results?q=myles+monroe

Chapter 8
1. 2 Timothy 1:6
2. 1 Samuel 17:46
3. 1 Samuel 17:37-40
4. 1 John 4:4
5. 1Chronicles 16:11
6. Nehemiah 8:10

7. Isaiah 40:29
8. 1 Samuel 22:30
9. 2 Chronicles 19:9

Chapter 9
1. 1 Peter 3:10-11
2. Isaiah 55:11
3. Romans 12:18
4. 1 Peter 3:12
5. Romans 12:9
6. 1 John 4:20
7. 1 John 4:8
8. Acts 10:34
9. Matthew 18:15-16
10. Ephesians 4:32
11. Mark 11:5
12. James 1:8
13. James 3:9-12
14. Deuteronomy 6:7
15. Philippians 3:17
16. Nehemiah 1:3-4
17. Merriam-Webster Online Dictionary. http://www.merriam-webster.com/dictionary/dualism?show=0&t=1399820157
18. Declaration of Independence. https://www.archives.gov/founding-docs/declaration-transcript
19. "What the World Needs Now." http://www.metrolyrics.com/what-the-world-needs-now-is-love-lyrics-jackie-deshannon.html

Chapter 10
1. James 3:4
2. John 10:10
3. 2 Chronicles 16:9
4. Nehemiah 2:17-18
5. James 4:14

6. Proverbs 27:1
7. John 9:15
8. 1 John 2:17
9. Ephesians 5:15-16
10. Romans 14;12
11. Ecclesiastes 8:15
12. Psalm 66:1
13. Lucado, Max. Max Lucado quotes at Brainy quote. Date unknown. November 2018. https://www.brainyquote.com/search_results?q=max+lucado
14. Wooden, John. John Wooden quotes at Brainy Quote. Date unknown. December 2018. https://www.brainyquote.com/search_results?q=john+wooden
15. Merriam Webster Online Dictionary. http://www.merriam-webster.com/dictionary/stewardship
16. Ingram, Chip. "Culture Shock." https://www.christianbook.com/culture-shock-personal-study-kit/pd/93221X?event=Christian-Authors|1006172

Chapter 11
1. Colossians 4:2
2. 1 Thessalonians 5:17
3. Luke 5:17
4. Luke 6:2
5. Matthew 14:23
6. Luke 22:39-41
7. John 17:3-5, 15-17
8. Mark 15:33-34
9. James 5:16
10. James 4:3
11. Psalm 66 :10
12. Proverbs 28:9
13. James 1:6-7
14. Ezekiel 14:5

15. Luther, Martin. Martin Luther quotes at Brainy Quote. Date unknown. December 2018. https://www.brainyquote.com/search_results?q=martin+luther
16. Matthew 6:15
17. 1 Peter 3:6-7
18. James 4:2

Chapter 12
1. Isaiah 55:11
2. Psalm 119:11
3. Proverbs 22:17-19
4. Acts 1:8
5. Psalm 119:24
6. Psalm 119:97
7. James 1:22-25

Chapter 13
1. 1 Thessalonians 4:1
2. Matthew 22:33
3. 1 Chronicles 21:24
4. Philippians 4:8
5. Romans 8:32
6. John 10:10
7. 2 Corinthians 4:7
8. Ecclesiastes 2:11
9. 2 Corinthians 4:7
10. Philippians 2:1
11. Romans 15:4
12. 1 Corinthians 4:20
13. Galatians 2:20
14. Philippians 2:13
15. John 15:5
16. Isaiah 26:3
17. Hebrews 9:2
18. Hebrews 6:18-19

19. John 13:7
20. Deuteronomy 23:14
21. Psalm 34:15
22. Merriam Webster Online Dictionary. http://www.merriam-webster.com/
23. dictionary/sacrifice
24. Lewis, C.S. "C.S. Lewis Quotes." Famous Quotes and Quotations at BrainyQuote. Date unknown. November 2018. http://www.brainyquote.com/quotes/authors/c/c_s_lewis.html
25. Ziglar, Zig. Zig Ziglar quotes at Brainy Quote. Date unknown. December 2018. https://www.brainyquote.com/search_results?q=zig+ziglar
26. Chan, Frances. "Frances Chan Quote." *http://www.brainyquote.com/quotes/authors/f/francis_chan.html*

Chapter 14
1. Jeremiah 2:13
2. Philippians 3:16-20
3. Philippians 3:12
4. James 1:23-25
5. Joshua 1:8
6. Pslam 119:11
7. Matthew 6:11
8. Romans 8:25
9. Mark 6:5-6
10. James 1:6-8
11. James 3:9-12
12. Einstein, Albert. Albert Einstein quotes at Brainy Quote. Date unknown. December 2018. https://www.brainyquote.com/search_results?q=albert+einsteinmes 3:9-12

CPSIA information can be obtained
at www.ICGtesting.com
Printed in the USA
BVHW031748260819
556836BV00005B/42/P